Project Management Crash Course

How To Successfully Manage Projects In Any Industry And Win Over Your Company And Customers

Umer W.

The PMBOK (Project Management Body of Knowledge) is published by the PMI (Project Management Institute). It provides global standards, processes, and guidelines for managing projects. This book focuses on learnings from the PMBOK and aims to make project management accessible for the masses.

Contents

Introduction

Hello and Welcome!

Thank you for taking the time to read this. After all, time has become such a valuable gift these days. I promise that when you're done reading, you will have a better way of approaching work. By learning these concepts, ideas and skills, you will be able to reach your professional, entrepreneurial, and personal goals faster.

Project management is a must have skill in the 21'st century. Companies reward employees who are adept at managing critical projects with higher salaries and faster promotions, while entrepreneurs find it vital for efficiently managing their teams and developing the next big world changing product/service. Also, by being more efficient at work, you will be able to get more done in lesser time, and hence create more space for yourself personally so that you can do what you love doing.

This book will help you hit the ground running by equipping you with the absolute essentials of Project Management. As you read through, you will develop a complete and clear picture of what a project is about, who are the people involved, and how you can successfully manage and deliver projects.

In my view, Project Management is an art that provides a path for how to get things done in the best and most optimized way possible. It helps us find our way in a world with increasingly complex systems and getting work done while dealing with a large number of people.

As a subject, project management can be challenging to absorb and requires significant time commitment. Most books are too complicated and don't immediately teach you the bottom line you're looking for: i.e. How do you manage a Project?

To address this, I extracted the most important concepts about managing projects and condensed them into this easy to read guide which you hold in your hands. With this book, I wanted to welcome everyone across the world from all backgrounds to project management. Therefore, I have used simple language for explanations so that you are able to absorb and apply the learnings quickly in your everyday work. Furthermore, I have intentionally used relatable examples and scenarios that will clarify your understanding of project management regardless of whichever industry you work in.

I am absolutely thrilled to have you here. Let us begin.

Umer W.

Book Overview - What you will Learn

The Main Content

At its core, the book discusses the main pillars of project management, known as Knowledge Areas. These knowledge areas are applicable to most Projects across multiple industries including IT, construction, engineering, finance, healthcare, and consulting, just to name a few.

Each knowledge area has been explained in two parts, the first shares the background of what the concept is, and the second teaches you the processes of how to implement that concept:

1. What is (e.g. What is Scope Management)

2. How to (e.g. How to Perform Scope Management)

Important Project Management Terms

Furthermore, you will also learn about the key terms, documents and topics that are important for every project manager to know about. To name a few, these include:

- What is a Business Case
- What is a Project Charter
- What are Constraints
- What is Historical Information
- What are Lessons Learned
- What are Risk Response Plans

-Plus several more.

Bonus Content - Being Greater

You will also find strategic level content focusing on making you a better project manager.

We will explore what exactly is the role of a project manager and what are the tasks and responsibilities you should expect to be involved in while managing projects in an organization.

Also, you will learn what are some of the biggest mistakes made while managing projects and how you can significantly increase the probability of your project's success and protect it against failure.

Additionally, you will learn what makes project managers indispensable, how you can manage your teams and how to be an invaluable resource for companies, enabling you to earn higher salaries and get shortlisted for faster promotions.

Understanding Project Management

What is a Project

We're going to learn about two important concepts. First, we're going to learn is what exactly is a project and secondly, we're going to learn about what is a deliverable.

So first, let's understand what exactly is a project. A project is a temporary endeavour. This means that it is not something that is ongoing, it is a one-off effort.

Secondly, a project is something that has a definite beginning and an end. So, it has a starting point and it has an ending point.

Lastly, a project is something which creates a unique product service or result. The emphasis here is on the aspect of a project being unique and delivering something that is one of a kind.

- A building
- Software application (e.g. iPhone or Android app)
- A Website
- A bridge

How do the examples above encompass the characteristics of a project?

Let's take the example of a bridge in a city. Firstly, constructing a bridge is a one-off venture, you will just have to build it once (hopefully), and it's not something you would have to work on every day, so developing the bridge is a temporary event. Also, it is unique since the bridge has a specific starting and ending point because it is connecting specific parts of the city. Furthermore, it has a unique design to make it aesthetically pleasing to look at. The same principles can be easily applied to the rest of the examples I've mentioned, think about how and why they can be considered projects.

Lastly, I'd recommend you apply the same principles to the work you do, what kind of projects have you worked on?

Next, let's take the example of a building as a project. We will use this to explain another important aspect of project management, known as a deliverable.

What is a Deliverable

The unique outcome which is produced by the project is known as the project deliverable. This can include any products you may develop, or services, or any type of result that came about as a result of doing the project. Therefore, a building in Manhattan, New York is a project. This is because each building will be built in a unique location that no other building can occupy, it will have its own specifications and requirements for raw materials and labour.

A Deliverable may also be considered as the Output of the project, i.e. what comes out of the project once you have carried it out.

It is also important to know that a project also has deliverables within itself. For example, the deliverables within the building project can be the floors, pillars, and the roof of the structure you're developing. The final deliverable of this project would be the overall completed building. On the other hand, everything that went into developing that building were also deliverables which were within that project.

Therefore, we can summarize the building project as follows:

Final Deliverable: A Completed Building

Deliverables Within the Project: Floor, Pillars, Roof

The Project Manager's Role on a Project

Who is the Project Manager and what does he/she do on the project?

Project Manager = PM

The project manager's role is a broad one. It cannot be simplified into any one specific task. Instead, think of the project manager as the master orchestrator of all that needs to be done to complete the project. To simplify things completely, the number one task of the project manager, is to communicate. The PM is the center around whom everything else happens and is the one person who knows what is happening on different parts of the project.

Let us bring clarity to the exact role and responsibilities of project managers and the actions they are involved in. We will learn what is expected of us and what we should be doing while managing projects:

Success or Failure

A Project Manager is the person who is responsible for the project, simply put, you are the project champion. You are the person selected by your company/organization to fulfill the project's objectives and to manage the project team. The PM is responsible for the success or failure of the project, this make or break responsibility rests on the PM's shoulders and is the bottom line of their performance.

Communication Skills

It is very important for the PM to have excellent communication skills. Over 90 percent of a PM's time is spent communicating between people, teams, and stakeholders. Your coordination with stakeholders relies on your ability to understand, develop, and share relevant information at the right time to make sure the project is going on track.

Leadership, Training, Negotiating, Coaching

You will be expected to spend your time performing leadership by providing direction to the project. You will build teams, get them to work together efficiently and provide the necessary training to develop their effectiveness. Also, you will be indulging in negotiations to acquire the best resources for the project. In case the project runs into problems, you will be managing conflict to resolve issues. Your team will rely on you for coaching and guiding them through the project.

Coordinating and getting work done through others

A strong project manager is the ultimate coordinator of people and resources. This is because you are responsible for getting work done through other people for the project. You coordinate the work between different departments, stakeholders and project team. I wanted to reiterate and highlight a key point here, remember that the project manager is not responsible for doing the project work by himself/herself. Instead, you get the project work done through other people and manage that work to ensure it is done the correct way and fulfills the requirements.

Developing schedule, budget and reserves

Given that projects operate in strict timelines, the PM is responsible for developing a realistic schedule. We say realistic since we need to allocate a reasonable time for how long it will take to perform each activity involved in doing the project work. You cannot be too stringent with the timing and neither can you be too generous with it, it needs to be just right, meaning realistic.

Next, developing the project budget is done by summing up all the costs on all the types of work involved on the project, and that is your project budget. In other words, add all the costs of all the type of work required to do the project, and you will have your budget. (Explained in more detail in Cost Management Chapter)

Furthermore, note that projects can go through changes or disturbances which can negatively affect your costs or schedule. You can't afford to go over your project budget and neither can you afford to have delays. To address this, project managers are responsible for creating reserves.

Reserves are like safety backups of time and money. The project manager allocates bits of extra time and money on the project to avoid address challenges or problems faced by the project. So, if your project is getting delayed by 10 days and if you already have a time reserve of 15 days, you can still afford to bear that delay since it will still meet the project deadline date.

Note that the reserves of time and money are included as a part of your budget and schedule and are not something you add later on when a problem occurs on the project.

Managing Human and Material Resources

Projects make use of skilled professionals and specialized equipment. The project manager is responsible for determining what resources are required for a project. On your own, you will be allocated certain resources in the form of a project team, however, projects can be complex and require multiple skillsets and resources. It is likely you will have to acquire resources from other parts of organization and from external vendors as the project advances.

Your aim would be to get the most optimal resources to work on your project. As a result, you will find yourself negotiating with department managers e.g. IT, Marketing, Engineering etc. to borrow their team members.

Furthermore, you will create job descriptions for project team members and stakeholders along with ensuring that roles and responsibilities are clearly assigned.

As the project work gets done, you will track the performance of the team members and evaluate the need for training. You may also create rewards and recognition systems for achieving project milestones to keep the morale and performance levels high across team members.

Performance Tracking

Since it is important to track the progress of the project, you are expected to measure project performance and identify any variances using specific performance metrics. Hence, before you start off with your project, it is important to decide through what means or measures will you use to evaluate the performance. E.g. is your project on developing a new car engine delivering the high-speed miles/hour or Km/Hour values that the engine was originally planned to deliver? So before you start the project, define the performance metrics.

Responding to Changes – Analyze Impact and Recommend Corrective Action

In today's fast paced environment of rapid product launches and ever evolving marketplace conditions, the project manager is expected to respond quickly to changes. Changes can be broad in nature, e.g. customer has asked for extra product features, the project deadline has been decreased, the project budget has been cut to 75% of the original amount etc.

It's important to note that changes are not implemented directly without analysis on the project. They are analyzed, and then are either accepted, or rejected. (Discussed in more detail later)

The project manager deals with changes on the project by analyzing the impact of the changes (what will be affected due to the change and by how much) and then recommending corrective actions (What can we do to set the project on the right track so that it still achieves its goal.

How projects are Started – What is the Business case

A business case gives the reasoning for starting the project. It explains the reason why a project was initiated in the first place and why it is worth taking up. It provides information on whether it is worthwhile making an investment in this project, whether it makes sense to spend money on this project and will it give the organization the appropriate returns.

Projects are mostly taken up to fulfill the needs of businesses, which can range from catering to market needs, to technological advancements. For example, an automobile manufacturer may want to launch a new product line of cars to increase sales and hence revenues and profitability. Or it may want to increase its productivity by upgrading its factory machinery, so it can produce more cars in lesser time. All these reasons may be considered as the business case for starting a project.

.

What are Process Groups

The management of any type of a project can be divided into five different process groups. Think of it as the flow or series of stages that your project needs to go through. Whenever you start a project, try to approach it as if you are going to segment its progression through different stages.

How does using process groups help us?

They help us organize the project and make it easier to manage. Things start to make a lot more sense when you put everything in its right place. Large projects can have numerous variables, and if you don't put them in order, you might risk project failure. Without order, projects can go into chaos.

- The process groups include:
- Initiating
- Planning
- Executing
- Monitoring and Controlling
- Closing

The project manager uses these process groups in order to manage and supervise the project.

Now let's try to understand each of these different process groups one by one.

Initiating

Initiating is mainly concerned with starting a project and developing the initial requirements in order to begin the project. So, initiating is about how you're going to start off with the project in the first place and what exactly do we require to make the project successful. Think of it as a very broad level overview of the entire project.

Planning

Planning is where you need to establish what are the things you need to do in order to get the project done. This is where you will define the course of action on how the project's objectives and requirements are going to be achieved. It is always recommended to spend more time in planning, the more thought you put into the planning, the smoother will be the execution and the lesser problems you will encounter. Think about how you're going to get the work done on the project and what risks can the project encounter. If you've covered these two aspects in the early stages, then you won't have to face problems later due to lack of planning or preparation.

Executing

Executing is concerned with getting the actual work done on the project in order to achieve its objectives. This is where you're getting work done through people and through material resources.

Monitoring and Controlling

Monitoring and Controlling includes tracking, reviewing and regulating the performance of the project. It is concerned with making sure that all of the work that is being done on the project is on track. In case there are any problems that are occurring on the project you need to make sure that you're implementing corrective actions in order to bring the project back on track as soon as possible.

Monitoring

When it comes to monitoring, this specifically refers to collecting, measuring and then analysing information related to the project's performance in order to identify variations. Variations refer to anything that is not going according to plan on the project.

14

Controlling

Controlling involves making sure that you're taking the right and appropriate corrective actions in order to bring the project performance back on track. In case you notice that the performance of the project is going off track, you need to implement the right corrective measures and make the right adjustments as per the original plan in order to make sure that the work is being done according to requirements and

Closing

Closing is all about finalizing all the activities and the work that is being done on the project and formally closing it. This is where you will wrap up all of the work done on the project.

Process groups help bring order to your project. Think of these process groups as a template which help you organize a project through its different stages.

What are Knowledge Areas

This is another one of the most important topics when it comes to project management. In simple terms, knowledge areas are like categories of knowledge based on which projects are managed.

For example, every project faces risks, every project has a time duration/schedule, costs, stakeholders etc. Hence, in order to help manage these different aspects of a project, these aspects are categorized as knowledge areas.

Each knowledge area has its own processes. The processes within each knowledge area include the guidelines through which a specific aspect of the project is managed. For example, the Risk Management knowledge area includes all the processes and guidelines which show how to manage Risk on a project. The same applies for the rest, e.g. the cost management knowledge area includes the processes and guidelines which show you how to manage costs on a project.

Overall, Projects are managed across 10 different knowledge areas which include:

- Integration Management
- Scope Management
- Schedule Management
- Cost Management
- Quality Management
- Resource Management
- Communications Management
- Risk Management
- Procurement Management
- and Stakeholder Management

Let's understand what each of those areas mean (Please note we will indeed cover all of these knowledge areas in more detail later, for now, it is very important to get an overhead perspective on what role does each play when it comes to managing projects.)

Integration management focuses on Integrating Processes across the project

It is concerned with identifying what sort of work is required to do the project and then integrating processes across the project with one another. Think of integration management as a way to make the different parts of the project work together.

Scope Management focuses on Developing Product Scope and Project Scope

For product scope, it covers what is included in the product you have to develop and what not to include in the product.

Similarly, for project scope, it covers what should be included in the work of the project and what is not included in the project work.

Schedule Management focuses on Developing Project Schedule

It includes coming up with the timelines and the Project Schedule. It also includes figuring out how much time each activity on the project will take.

How much time is this project going to take? When do we start it? When do we end it? How much time is it going to take in order to complete the different activities which are involved in the project. So you will use all of that information to develop the schedule of the project.

Cost Management is all about estimating the costs which will be incurred on the project. It focuses on Estimating costs for human resources and material resources

For example, if you have engineers working on the project, then what are going to be the costs on the project with regards to human resources or the people working on the project.

It also includes coming up with the cost of material resources, which includes the cost of the material used on the project. E.g. if you are using different types of materials for example if you are constructing a building, what will be the cost of the steel and cement.

Quality Management focuses on Ensuring Product Quality and Process Quality

Firstly, for product quality, it ensures that the quality of the products being created is at an acceptable level.

Secondly for process quality, it ensures that the processes of project management itself are at an acceptable level.

For example, if you're developing a software product, then you want to make sure that the quality of the deliverable, meaning the product quality is of a certain standard. You also want to ensure that the processes being used to develop that IT software product are of an acceptable quality.

Therefore, both the quality of your processes and of the products that need to be of a certain standard.

Resource Management focuses on Acquiring, Developing and Managing People and Material Resources

It involves getting the right people to work on the project, developing them, and then managing their performance.

It also involves getting the right material resources and equipment to do the project work at the right time when it is required on the project.

Communication Management focuses on Providing Right information to the right people at the right time

It ensures that the right kind of information reaches the right kind of people in a timely and efficient manner.

Risk Management focuses on Dealing with Opportunities and Threats

Risks can be of two different types. You can have positive risks which are known as opportunities and then you can have negative risks which are known as threats.

You need to ensure that opportunities on the project are capitalized on and threats to the project are taken care of. This involves developing specific plans to deal with opportunities and threats.

Procurement Management focuses on Purchasing Goods, Managing Contracts

It involves purchasing goods or services which you require on the project from external stakeholders like vendors and suppliers.

Since you're dealing with a large number of buyers and suppliers, you also need to make sure you're managing those contracts the in the correct way.

Stakeholder Management focuses on Taking care of stakeholders needs

It involves taking care of the different stakeholders involved on the project and looking after their needs and interests regarding the project.

Any single project can have a large number of different stakeholders and each one of them can have very different expectations from the project.

So, stakeholder management is all about how you actually meet those expectations and how are you able to engage with those stakeholders

The difference between knowledge areas and process groups

So, you might be thinking what is the difference between process groups and knowledge areas?

To keep it easy and simple, i'd like you to think of process groups as the different stages that a project goes through all the way from initiating to closing the project.

On the other hand, think of knowledge areas as the tools which you will use in order to manage the project.

Knowledge Areas are about specialized areas of knowledge that are used on project management topics, whereas Process Groups apply that knowledge.

While knowledge areas provide expertise on a specific area to help manage a project, the process groups are the means through which that knowledge is applied on a project.

How to Manage Teams – Best Practices and Must Do's

In this section I'm going to share my top suggestions for managing teams. Once the project starts, ideally speaking you want your team members to consistently perform like a well-oiled machine with a clear goal without getting derailed. These tips will help you ensure your team members are able to deliver high productivity, avoid problems due to miscommunications/lack of understanding, support one another and solve problems faster.

Develop Clarity of scope

Providing clarity in terms of exactly what work is supposed to be done on the project can go a long way in developing team effectiveness. Each person on the team needs to be completely clear on:

- What is the project
- What are the project's objectives?
- What needs to be done to complete the project

Develop Clarity of Responsibility

Now that you've made it clear what the project is about, it is vital to let people know what their role is on the project. People need to know:

- What tasks are they responsible for
- How can they accomplish the tasks they are responsible for
- Who are they working with and whom can they ask for assistance or support

Develop Team member Onboarding and Problem Resolution Guidelines

Do you remember the first time you started working at your new job? Everyone comes across challenges and problems during work, and depending on different cultures, people may find it embarrassing to ask for help. This is especially true for bigger companies where new hires can especially feel lost because they've just joined in and don't know their way around the place or the people.

Oftentimes, we take for granted that people will work their way around problems. However, these activities can waste time and create undue stress. It would be far more beneficial to help your team member get their actual project work done rather than set them on an adventure to find out in what department does John from the legal team sit so that they could get "X" document from him.

Before the beginning of every project, deliver a detailed overview for the organization, the most relevant resources they would need to engage with, the people will likely interact with, the documents/materials they are likely to make use of, and have a detailed onboarding session with your team members.

Get Buy in

Once people are clear on the scope and responsibilities on the project, it is important to get their Buy in. Getting people to state their Buy in for the project is akin to having them acknowledge that yes we understand the project, it's requirements, and we agree to our roles and responsibilities.

Develop Milestones

To track project progress, the team needs to know how far it has come to be able to evaluate its performance.

Setting up daily/weekly/monthly milestones can help make your progress transparent and help you determine how to best manage the project moving forward.

You can ask the following to determine how well you're doing on the project with your team:

- What work has been completed and what is still left over, have we completed a sufficient percentage of the work as planned or are we lagging behind in delivery?
- Are we over budget or under budget/How much have we spent, can we still complete the project with the money left
- Are we ahead of schedule or behind schedule, How much time do we have left, can we complete it in the remaining time

Establish Ground Rules

Ground rules are the basic mode of operation or guidelines based on which the team would operate. It is a code of conduct which the team is supposed to abide by. Ground rules can help teams maintain employee satisfaction and performance levels while avoiding undesirable behaviours/actions that can harm the project.

How meetings would be conducted

Setting ground rules for meetings can help avoid wasting time and making uninformed decisions.

Ground rules can differ from manager to manager and from one company culture to the other. I have found the following method and flow to be useful:

- Specify the topics of discussion and meeting agenda
- Each team member shares their points of discussion beforehand to all meeting members

- All members become aware of discussion points (progress updates from each member) and challenges being faced
- Actual meeting does not dwell on basics and focuses instead on solutions to problems
- Meeting members share solutions and constructive feedback
- Repeat for next meeting

Having an agenda of discussion points distributed to all the meeting members can ensure that everyone knows the basics. The discussion can then move forward towards more productive decision-making conversations.

Prohibiting the usage of cell phones during presentations can ensure the members are respected and their points are well understood.

Delivering constructive feedback instead of criticism is vital. Members of the meeting should be encouraged to share thoughts on solving problems instead of fostering hostility between each other. There really is no point in bashing a team member, it just contributes to making the workplace more toxic. Instead, to put it simply, it's better to focus on where we stand today, what do we need to do to go where we want to go. With this approach, you can actually focus on the challenges a certain team member is facing and the members can then advise/offer support on overcoming them.

What are acceptable and unacceptable behaviours

Setting ground rules for managing interpersonal conflict can help improve team bonding and relationships.

Set up rules to be followed for managing conflict i.e., in case a problem occurs, how does a team member initiate the conversation?

Project teams can be diverse with people from multiple nationalities, races and religions working together. A happy workplace leads to more productivity and the way your team members treat each other will depend on what kind of environment you build.

Encourage a positive and supportive culture that respects diversity. For example, banning personal comments (I hate your work) in favour of fact-based feedback (Please increase the speed of the software application by 10%) can help avoid conflicts and maintain a professional environment.

How to Transform from being a Good Project Manager to a Great Project Manager

What can you do to be more successful than the average project manager?

For this section, let's assume that every project manager is great at getting projects done within the budget and schedule. How do you stand out from the rest and yourself irreplaceable? What quality can you have that cannot be replicated easily by others?

To explain this, I wanted to return to a statement I mentioned earlier i.e,90 percent of a project manager's time is spent communicating.

I'd like you to think about that for a second.

Now ask yourself the following questions:

- Do people like working with you?
- Would your project team willingly and gladly go the extra mile in ensuring your deliverables are top notch?
- Would functional managers be willing to do lend you their top resources at a call's notice?

Your project performance is tied to the quality of your relationships. And the quality of your relationships will depend on how well you are able to communicate. You are that one person with whom everyone else is connected. Your project team members look to you for guidance. The more your team likes and respects you, the harder they will work. The more pleasant and responsive you are in looking after your customers needs, the more likely it is that they will give you more business in the future. The more reliable and dependable you are for your senior management, the more likely it is that you will get to work on better projects.

Be the person who brings people together

As you manage projects across your career, focus on developing good working relationships such that people look forward to working with you.

Take time to understand the people involved on the project. Think about people's goals. What are the goals of your project team, what are the goals of your suppliers, can you help them achieve these goals without compromising the boundaries of the project?

Network across departments, get to know people on the legal team, marketing, finance, HR, supply chain, vendors, suppliers, customers.

Gradually, this network of people you know inside and outside your organization will make you the "Go To" guy. Anytime something unique needs to get done, people will come to you because they know you're connected with various people who are specialists in their fields.

You can always replace skills, there will always be someone who can outdo your performance. However, it is not easy to replace the personal and valuable social networks you develop while working.

How to Minimize Project Failure - Avoid Rework, Plan Proactively, Develop Clarity

Have you ever been in a situation where you completed your work and were pleasantly informed that you have to do it all over again because there have been changes? How did that make you feel?

There's a reason that heading is in Capitals. Rework is the bane of projects. Having to do things over repeatedly can increase your costs and lead you to go over budget, delay your schedule and make you miss deadlines, and wear out your project team, all of which can increase the possibility of project failure.

This is not to suggest you should not expect changes to happen on the project, they are bound to happen and can be requested at any point of the project. Perhaps it might be your customer who demand extra features in the software, your senior management might demand that the project be completed earlier than its scheduled completion date, or even by your own hand if you feel the project performance needs to be tweaked.

However, it is the redoing of work you have already completed that is troublesome for the project. If you have to go back to the drawing board, this means you did not define the scope appropriately enough earlier.

What we want to eliminate, is the possibility of unnecessary changes that take place as a result of lack of preparation and foresight. Problems occur when you have to shift mid project and make changes that can mess up the entire project. Projects are not isolated, they are connected pieces and when one piece takes damage, its ripples are felt across the entire body.

So what can you do about this?

Develop clarity about the project. Collect information about it as exhaustively as you can at the beginning of the project. The more you know and the earlier you know, the better.

Plan ahead, figure out your entire scope of work as exhaustively as you can.

What are the different tasks we need to do?

What people do we need?

How much time do we need to do each part of the work?

What problems do we expect to face?

You may refer to the Project Charter to learn more about what information you should seek regarding the project. For each of the points listed in the charter, try to break them down into as much detail as possible before starting the project.

When you know exactly what you're supposed to do to complete the project, congratulations, you've just made life easier for yourself and the rest of the team. Your team members will love you for your clarity. When they know exactly what they're supposed to do, they will be able to figure out their own strategy on how to do that piece of work most productively. This will help them plan out their day and the rest of the week, allowing them to recharge by dividing work appropriately between their personal life and work.

Don't let your team's hard work go to waste. Respect their time and your own.

Importance of Historical Information and Lessons Learned for Project Managers

While working on projects, organizations collect the information and knowledge that was created as a result of the project. For example, if it is a software product, all the information regarding its product including design, code, people who worked on it, what challenges were faced, what solutions were implemented, will be collected. This information will then be stored and made available for use for future projects.

This practice is highly valuable since it makes it convenient to understand and replicate approaches for projects that are similar in nature. No longer do you have to start everything from scratch since a lot of the relevant knowledge would be available to you through the experiences and learnings from past projects.

This information is especially useful in situations where you have recently joined a new organization.

You can request for information regarding past projects, this will help you quickly come up to speed with how the organization works, how previous projects were handled, and what information you can use for your future project. You do not have to start everything from scratch. If there is a workable solution for a known problem, then, there is no need to reinvent the wheel again. Take what you can use and get your project off the ground asap.

This information collected during projects can be divided into Lessons Learned and Historical Information.

As a project manager, you will be responsible for collecting and developing the historical information and lessons learned from your project. Lessons Learned and Historical Information are unique project learning's which are collected as the project progresses and are stored in the Organizational Knowledge Repositories so that they may be used in the future, on the same project, or on future projects. They are collected so that readymade solutions to problems may be available for use on future projects.

Next, let's explore how historical information and lessons learned differ from one another.

Historical Information

Historical information consists of information from past projects. It contains facts and information such as: What resources were used on the project, what were the costs of the raw materials, what are the product specifications etc.

As a best practice, you should review historical information whenever a new project is starting and use it in planning new projects

For projects which share a similar nature, historical information can help save a lot of time, effort and resources.

For example, if you were starting a new project, and information from a previous project of the same nature was available, think about how helpful that would be to your new project. You would have access to useful facts such as:

- What were the cost estimates
- What specific resources were used
- What sort of skills were required
- What risks did the project have
- What was the project management plan like

All this information would help make it easier for you to succeed in your new project.

Historical information is especially used for estimating, risk management and project planning.

Lessons Learned

Lessons learned contain the Learning's and knowledge gained from the project.

Knowledge gained on the project refers to two important aspects:

1. How was the project handled (What went right on the project, what went wrong on the project)

2. What could be done to improve performance in the future

Lessons learned involves the collection of approaches learned during the project. For example, how were the risks handled, how were problems resolved, what actions helped the project be successful etc. Lessons learned are collected by the stakeholders as the project progresses. The stakeholders are the most appropriate people who can complete the lessons learned since e.g. an engineer would know best about his own part of the work on the project, the problems he dealt with and how he was able to solve them. Hence, it is not just the project manager who is involved in collecting lessons learned.

Hence, as a project manager, it is vital that you review lessons learned before starting a new project.

Work Performance Data, Work Performance Information, Work Performance Reports

Work Performance Data

Work Performance Data refers to the measurements taken from activities which are done during project work. Simply speaking, these are the basic numbers you will receive related to the project i.e. the raw data of the project's performance.

Examples:

- How much money has been spent on the project
- What is the percentage completion status of the project
- How any defects are there on the product
- What are the starting and finishing dates of activities

Work Performance Information

Once you receive the raw numbers and data from the project, you then analyze that information in context of the project. When work performance data is analyzed and interpreted, it becomes work performance information.

It is an organized summary of work performance data and provides information on the progress and status of the project.

WPI involves comparing and using different data points to understand how well we are doing on the project and what story do the numbers tell us. You're going to analyze the numbers and compare the planned performance versus the actual performance of the project.

Examples:

- What is the cost performance of the project, analyze the planned cost versus actual cost spent
- How effective was the risk response plan against the risks we identified?

- Given the current project status, what are the forecasted estimates to complete it? How much time do we require and how much would it cost?

Work Performance Reports

These are the presentations and status reports that contain information about the performance of the project. They are developed using work information. You can consider these as a vital instrument that you will distribute to shareholders to keep them updated about the project's progress.

So basically, this is the WPI converted into a presentable format with graphs, dashboards etc. for management and relevant stakeholders.

To summarize, work performance data is analyzed and interpreted to be developed into work performance information, this work performance information is then developed into work performance reports which are then sent out to the project stakeholders to keep them abreast of the project's status.

Understanding Stakeholders

Stakeholders are an integral part of project management. You will spend your time in project management dealing with all sorts of stakeholders from different backgrounds. Some will be nice, some not so. Your understanding of who stakeholders are, what is important to them, who are the most important stakeholders, how can they impact your project, and how you should manage them will determine your project's success.

- Stakeholders refer to all the People Or Organizations involved in the project.
- They may be internal or external to the organization, for example they can be someone from within your team or another department. Or they can be from another company such as a supplier or a vendor.
- They can either have an active role by being directly involved in the project or they can have an advisory role where they provide advice because of their expertise since a lot of stakeholders are subject matter experts. Subject matter experts are people who have specialized knowledge in a specific area.
- Stakeholders can be positively or negatively affected as a result of the project. So whenever you're doing a project, try to evaluate whether there is anyone who can be negatively effected by your project. For example, do you need to borrow engineers from a team that is already busy with their own work?
- Similarly, Stakeholders can also influence a project positively or negatively. For example, if a stakeholder is an expert in engineering, they can help you develop your tech product faster and more thoroughly. On the flip side, if the stakeholder is resistant to your project, e.g. if the engineering manager is not willing to let you borrow his team members for your project, this can result in your project being delayed. Therefore, influence needs to be managed by the project manager for the project to be successful.

Types of Stakeholders

Next, let's look at some of the major types of stakeholders you can frequently expect to interact with during the project:

Sponsor

Think of the sponsor as the main supporter of the project. He/She is mostly a senior manager or executive who plays a leadership role while being accountable for the project. The sponsor provides resources, funding and rounds up support in the organization to get the project off the ground. Most importantly, the sponsor gives the project manager authority for the project. Giving authority means that it allows the project manager to start the project using funds, resources and authority in an official capacity as a project manager.

They can also act as a spokesperson for the project for the higher management. As a project manager, if you ever come across a problem that you do not have the official authority to solve, you may seek help from the sponsor.

Project Team

The project team refers to the people who are involved in performing the work and creating the deliverables of the project to achieve its objectives. They are responsible for completing the project work within the budget and while adhering to schedule milestones and timelines. They may consist of both full time and part time resources. The project team also helps the project manager in sharing information on risks and status updates.

Functional Managers

The managers for specific departments who manage their own teams and resources e.g. IT, Finance, Supply Chain, Product Development. It is likely you will be borrowing their team members for your projects as a PM.

Customers

People or organizations who will receive the final product of the project. Customers can be internal from within your work organization i.e. a separate department e.g. If an IT department is working on developing a customer service software for the marketing department, then they are your internal customer.

Customers may also be external, which includes other companies or individuals who are buying from you in the marketplace.

Sellers

External companies, i.e. contractors or suppliers who provide services, resources and items to the organization performing the project.

How to manage stakeholder expectations

Let's look at what does it mean to manage stakeholder expectations:

- Firstly, it is very important know the requirements, needs and expectations of all stakeholders. It is vital that you address and satisfy the requirements of stakeholders on the project, e.g., the client of the project, your chief engineer who is developing the product.
- Secondly you should keep stakeholders informed about the project on a regular basis. This can help you get feedback in case the project starts going off track.
- You should know the key decision makers and individuals in an organization and understand their needs to increase the chances of project success. Furthermore, the needs of the stakeholders should be addressed in order of priority.

- Note that you cannot satisfy every stakeholder, therefore the most important ones are satisfied on a higher priority, for example, the customer is usually prioritized over all others when it comes to deciding which stakeholder's need should be addressed first and foremost.

How to Involve Stakeholders on The Project – The Complete Overview

Stakeholders are such an important part of project management, most of your time will be spent dealing with people and getting work done while ensuring it is done the right way. I wanted to make sure to give you a walkthrough of the most important considerations with stakeholders while managing your project. Moreover, I will still cover the stakeholder management processes in a later section as well, however, before that, I'd like to help you develop a simple and effective perspective on how to involve stakeholders:

Identify all the stakeholders:

Firstly, it is of utmost priority to identify all the stakeholders as early as possible at the beginning of the project. This helps the project in avoiding unnecessary risk later.

Secondly, it is necessary to determine as many requirements of the stakeholders as possible. This involves determining their Interests, Influence and expectations.

Discuss the stakeholder's requirements with them and then set realistic expectations for which requirements will be met and which will not be met.

Remember that the more complete the requirements are, the more are the chances that the project will succeed at fulfilling the stakeholder's requirements and increase the chances of project success.

Discover Stakeholder's expectations

After identifying all the stakeholders, the project manager should know what expectations and concerns the different stakeholders have from the project.

Now what are expectations you might ask? Expectations include those concerns that stakeholders might have running in their minds but that haven't been shared explicitly with you.

Expectations should be discussed, analyzed and converted into project requirements as soon as possible.

Remember that the more specific the project requirements, the more realistically you will be able to evaluate project performance.

Determine Stakeholder Interests

Next, it is important to Determine the interests of the stakeholders in order to keep them engaged with the project.

Once you know a stakeholder's interests, you can either incorporate them within the project, or develop them as a reward.

For instance, certain stakeholders working on the project might want to develop a certain skillset. For example, engineers working on the project might want to improve their project management skills. You can increase the engineer's level of involvement in the project by promising to reward them by sending them for project management training.

Identify the level of influence of the stakeholders

Next, it is very important to identify the level of influence each stakeholder. Stakeholders can positively or negatively exert influence on the project, so knowing this information will clarify how to handle different people to make the project succeed without problems.

This will allow you to develop plans on how to manage the stakeholders in order to capitalize and gain support from the stakeholders who can positively influence the project and address the concerns of the stakeholders who can influence the project negatively.

Next, determine the level of involvement of the stakeholders in the project, meaning when will they be involved and to what extent will they be involved.

It is a good idea involve stakeholders by making use of their expertise on the project, involve them according to what they are good at.

Stakeholder Interaction Summary

Next, we are going to go over a quick and brief overview to summarize your interaction with stakeholders:

Plan Stakeholder Management

This process includes how you will manage the interests, expectations and influence of the stakeholders and keep them involved with the project.

Plan communications with stakeholders.

The project manager needs to ensure that stakeholders are communicated with effectively throughout the duration of the project. Planning communications with stakeholders ensures information reaches them in a efficient, effective and timely fashion.

Managing stakeholders influence, expectations and engagement

This refers to Managing stakeholder engagement across the life of the project so that problems do not occur while the project is in progress.

Constant Communication with stakeholders

Which refers to keeping stakeholders involved and updated via reports, presentations, and updates.

Control Stakeholder Engagement and Communications

This refers to Identifying Gaps in communication with stakeholders and addressing them immediately.

Integration Management and The Project Charter

What is Integration Management

Integration management refers to integrating the processes of the project and getting them to work together. In other words, it refers to getting the various parts and elements of the project to work together in a smooth manner.

Most importantly, it involves understanding and managing all the different types of knowledge areas simultaneously. This includes managing all the knowledge areas including Scope, Cost, Schedule, Quality, HR, Communications, Risk, Procurement and Stakeholder Management.

Consider it this way, a project manager must balance all the knowledge areas at the same time since each knowledge area will have an effect on one another (We will discuss why this is so in an example soon).

Integration management is the main role of the project manager, it is about understanding how the various components of the project fit together and how to manage them.

At the same time, integration management is the only knowledge area which is done across all the different process groups, meaning all the way from initiating to closing the project. The project manager is responsible for managing all the different components of a project and then juggling them together as a single complete object.

This is the essence of a project managers main responsibility.

Now let's talk about an example of how integration management can be done on the project and how different processes can be integrated together. For example, if you're constructing a building as a project, and you want to increase the quality of its rooms. Increasing the quality of the rooms would likely mean you would have to use better equipment, better labour/skills/human resources and of course it would also result in increased costs.

Hence, you must consider what changes will be required to the schedule, resources and cost for improving the quality. It is important to consider the effect on the knowledge areas (schedule management, resource management and cost management) before you can actually go about increasing the quality.

Now let's take another example of an IT product.

When adding new features to website or a software application, consider whether those changes are within the scope. If those changes are not within the scope, then what will be the impact of the additional extra features. You would especially want to consider the impact of adding those extra features on the scope, time, cost and risks related to the project.

Therefore, before adding any new features, you must consider what would be the impact on the knowledge area as a result of adding new features to your website/software application. By how much would it increase the amount of work (Scope)? Would it increase the time to build the final product (Schedule)? What would be the risks of adding those new features, do we risk having to deal with software bugs (Risk Management)?

Therefore, it is important to consider that when you're conducting integration management, you must consider the project altogether and take into account the impact on all of the different knowledge areas.

Now let's look at what are the different processes of integration management.

Integration Management includes the following processes:

- Develop Project Charter
- Developed project management plan
- Direct and manage project work
- Manage project knowledge
- Monitor and control project work
- Perform integrated change control
- Close project

How to Make Changes and Manage Change Requests on Projects

Changes are inevitable in a project's life. They can occur due to several different reason's and can be requested from any stakeholder. If you are just starting off with managing project's, I'd like to clarify something before you get yourself into trouble: Please know that you cannot just go about making changes instantly or abruptly on the project. There is a proper guideline that needs to be followed through, which we will discuss shortly.

Changes on projects are initiated by submitting a change request. As the name suggests, a change request is just that, it is an official request for the project manager to implement a change on the project. You will receive requests to make changes through emails, during meetings/presentations, on the phone etc.

Also, it's important to note that when you receive a request for a change, it is necessary to first evaluate the effect and impact it would have on the project. Once they've been evaluated, then, the change can either be accepted or rejected.

Types of Changes on Projects:

Let's look at some common examples of changes on projects:

Market Changes

New Product Launch Scenario:

If your competitor has launched their product earlier than expected, you would now have to speed up the project to launch your own product at the earliest. Since you don't want your competitor getting the dominant market share, you would end up implementing a change by decreasing the schedule and increasing the number of resources to complete the project faster. As a result, the impact of the change would include higher costs and a decreased schedule.

Changes in Technology

New technology shift scenario:

You own a game development studio and mid-way through your new game project, you decide that you want to make your game playable in Virtual Reality as well. This means you would now have to get resources who specialize in developing VR games to help you develop the new functionality. This change results in an increase in scope, costs, and schedule.

Changes requested by the customer

Additional features scenario:

Customers can often request changes on projects. What is important to figure out is, whether the changes fit into the existing scope or not. Clients may often request additional features which will not be a part of the original scope that was decided. Adding ON to the existing scope means that you now have to go back and redo your baselines. Since the development of new features would require additional work, it is likely your scope baseline would include new deliverables, the schedule will expand since you now require more time, and your costs will increase because of the extra materials / skilled experts you require to develop the new feature.

Remember, it is vital to have the customer agree on your initial planned scope, the customer should acknowledge the deliverables that were originally planned. In case the client does demand additional features, they will know their request goes over and above the original scope.

However, in case the client's request is within the planned scope, then those features are to be included without changes to the baselines.

Walkthrough of how to make changes

Now let's go over step by step how to implement changes on projects:

1. You will receive a request to make changes on the project

Once you've received a change request, you now want to get detailed information about the nature and specifications of the change. It is important to understand what exactly is the nature of the change being requested and then discuss with the stakeholder to make sure you're on the same page. It is in your best interest to get all the information in an official Change request form. Once you've gathered that information, it is always a good practice to once again run that information by the person who initiated the change to develop a common understanding of what is required.

Most importantly, it is important to ensure you get the initiators official buy-in and acknowledgement that yes this is the exact description of the type of change they are requesting. This will protect you from a lot of potential problems that can occur due to miscommunication or misunderstandings.

2. Analyze the impact of the change on the project

Next, it is important to evaluate and analyze the impact of the change. You need to know what will be the result of the impact on the project constraints (the project constraints include Cost, Schedule, Scope, Customer Satisfaction, and Risk).

Most importantly, you should analyze the impact of the change on the triple constraint. The triple constraint includes scope, cost and schedule and these are considered the most important constraints of the project.

3. Approval or Rejection of Change Request

After evaluating the change request for its impact, you will make the decision to either implement or reject the change. Changes are reviewed by the Change Control Board, think of it as a committee who is responsible for evaluating the change and deciding whether to implement it or not. This committee can include different important stakeholders from the project including:

- Project Manager
- Experts
- Project Sponsor
- Functional Managers
- Customers

For small changes like adjustments, you have the discretion as the project manager to take a decision since those are well within your authority. However, for larger and higher impact changes that can considerably change the scope, budget and schedule, you will have to consult the Change control board, especially the sponsor and customer.

Changes that are within the planned scope are more easily implemented, for example this could include changes made to the project to bring it back on track.

In case of changes that are out of scope e.g. adding extra features to a software, these would require you to make significant changes to the project documents.

Which leads us to our next point-

4. Update the project documents

Once you accept the change request, it is now time to document these changes. The project documents will be updated to reflect the new specifications of the project. The project management plan and baselines (scope, schedule, cost) need to reflect the changes, including, what new work needs to be done, what would be the additional costs, and how much more time is required to complete the project as a result of the change request.

In case the documents are not updated, people would end up working on different versions of the project which could lead to further problems. The goal is to ensure that everyone is working on the same version of the project. Therefore, from this point onward, everyone will be working on the revised version of the Project Management Plan and Project baselines.

5. Communicate and spread the word about the changes

Now that you've updated the project documents, it's important to inform everyone involved on the project regarding the changes. Your project team, senior management, and any other relevant stakeholders should be made aware of any updates to the project. If people are left out of this communication, it can be detrimental to the health of the project. So you need to help ensure they know about what's going on so that they can adjust make any required adjustments to their work as appropriate.

What is a Project Charter – Define Project Charter Process

The Project Charter is a document that describes the entire project. It gives you a complete high-level perspective on what the project is about, and everything related to it. This is your Go To document when it comes to managing the project.

Contents of the Project Charter

The project charter contains information regarding:

- What are Objectives and Goals
- What is the Business Case
- What is the Project Description
- What are the Project Requirements
- What is the Product Scope
- Who is the Project Manager
- What is the Success and Acceptance Criteria
- What are the Constraints
- What are the Risks
- What are the Milestones
- Who are the Stakeholders
- What are the Assumptions
- What is the Initial Budget
- What is the Initial Schedule

Develop Project Charter Process

A Project charter is developed by identifying stakeholders and discussing the major information points of the project. The way to create a project charter is to talk to all the stakeholders who will be involved with the project and from those discussions you will create the important information points of the project. Then, as a result of the discussions with stakeholders, the contents of the project charter are developed.

Important things to note about the Project Charter

- The first thing to know is that a project charter is a document which describes the project on an initial and overall level. What do I mean when I say the project charter describes the project on initial and overall level? I'd like you to think of the project charter as a short but cohesive and logical summary of all the important aspects of the project. Also note that the project charter is written before you actually start the project.

- According to the PMBOK, The project charter authorizes the existence of the project. It also authorizes the project manager to use resources (monetary, human, material) to get the project done. Simply speaking, the project charter makes the project official and brings it into existence so that work can start on the project.

- The charter plans the project at a high level, and contains the major points of information of a project, it also contains the Broader details of the project

- The creation of a project charter is a way to get the support of the senior management by making them accept and commit to the existence of the project.

- A project charter contains the goals and objectives, what is the success criteria, what are the high-level requirements, and what are the high-level risks and constraints the project is expected to face, what assumptions are we making etc.

- Anyone who reads the project charter should immediately be able to get an idea what the project is about and what are the most important things to know about it.

- It's important to know that the Project Charter is not a document that contains in depth detail, instead, the project is planned in detail only after the signing of the project charter. The reason that the charter does not contain a lot of detail is because detailed planning takes more time and costs more money, so detailed planning only starts once the project charter gets signed by senior management.

- Furthermore, we should keep in mind that The Project Charter is signed by the sponsor of the project or by senior management.
- Also, note that the project manager may or may not create the project charter. The sponsor may ask the project manager to create the charter or the charter may already have been created before the project manager is brought on board to manage the project.

Project Charter Template

Here is a sample template for a Project Charter. I'd like you to consider the project you're working on and try filling out the information in the different sections.

Business Need/Business Case – (Why is the Project required)
Project Description (What is the Project about, How will it be carried out)
Project Scope (What work is required to do the project)
Key Deliverables (What would be the outputs of the project)
Project Objectives (What key things do we expect to achieve, What is the Success Criteria)
Stakeholders Who will be involved in the project and who will be affected by it
Budget (How much do we expect the Project to Cost)

Schedule (How much time would it take to complete the project)
Milestones (What are the key measurable achievements and progress objectives of the project)
Constraints (What can hinder progress on the project)?
Risks (What High level Risks can the Project face)

How to Perform Integration Management

Now that you've learned about how to develop the project charter, let's move on to the next process of integration management, which is how to develop the project management plan.

Develop Project Management Plan Process

The project management plan is a document which contains all of the individual management plans along with the baselines of the product. So, what exactly does that mean? When it comes to the different knowledge areas, let's recall them to refresh our memory:

- Integration Management Plan
- Scope Management Plan
- Schedule Management Plan
- Cost Management Plan
- Quality Management Plan
- Resource Management Plan
- Communications Management Plan
- Risk Management Plan
- Procurement Management Plan
- Stakeholder Management Plan

What is a Management Plan?

All of these different management plans contain the strategy for managing the processes of the project. So as a project manager you need to develop a separate management plan for each of these knowledge areas.

Now what exactly are the different sections of a management plan. There are three main sections you need to take into account.

Sections of a Management Plan

- Planning
- Executing
- Controlling

Planning

First, let's talk about Planning. The Planning section of a management plan defines the processes and procedures which are to be followed for a specific knowledge area. For example, the planning section of the quality management plan will tell you what are the different processes and procedures that you need to have on the project in order to ensure quality on the project.

Similarly, when it comes to the planning section of our risk management plan, it will tell you about the different processes and procedures that you need to ensure on the project to manage risks on the project.

Executing

Next is executing. The executing section will tell you about how exactly you are supposed to go about doing the processes and procedures which you defined during planning. So to keep it simple, think about it this way, The planning section is going to tell you about the "What" and the executing section is going to tell you about the "How".

When it comes to planning quality, it will tell you what you're supposed to do on the project in order to ensure quality, and the executing section is going to tell you how exactly you are going to implement the plan and the procedures and the processes to implement quality.

Controlling

Lastly, let's discuss the controlling section of a management plan. Controlling will tell you how to analyse the performance of the project. It will also tell you about how to identify variances, e.g. if you notice the project is going off track, how can you bring the performance back on track.

That wraps up our discussion about Management Plans. To summarize, just remember that the Project Management Plan is a collection of all the individual management plans for the different knowledge areas.

Direct and Manage Project Work Process

This is the process in which the project manager is going to get work done on the project. These are tasks that you will be involved in doing during the project. E.g. this includes producing deliverables, meaning you're getting the work done by the team and they're going to be creating the deliverables of the project.

You will also be involved in gathering information from all the project work that is happening around you to make sure you keep track on its progress. Furthermore, you will be involved in getting changes done on the project in case they are required or requested. Lastly, you will be managing all of the different team members and the stakeholders who are involved on the project.

Manage Project Knowledge Process

As a project manager you're responsible for constantly making improvements to the project in order to ensure its success. Furthermore, you also need to undertake steps so that you can avoid failure. Management of the knowledge which is created on the project is a very critical factor when it comes to the responsibility of the project manager.

Firstly, you can use the knowledge from past projects in order to guide the execution of your current and future projects. Also, have discussions with the stakeholders or your project team members on how they worked on the previous projects which were of a similar nature to the one that you're working on right now.

You should use the knowledge and learnings from the previous projects. Talk to your team members on how they executed the projects in the past. Researching knowledge from past projects and from different stakeholders can help guide you in developing the execution plan for your current and future projects.

Furthermore, it is also your responsibility to create knowledge regarding your future and your current projects. Consider all of the things that are happening, the conflicts and problems that you're facing, the opportunities that you're capitalizing on, and the good things that you're executing on the project. All these factors should be taken into account and recorded so that somebody in the future can make use of them. Therefore, you will collect the knowledge, practices, and information regarding your current project and record it, and that is what Managing Project Knowledge is about.

Monitor and Control Project Work Process

As Project Manager, you should be tracking, reviewing and reporting the progress of the project on a continuous basis. This is because it is very important to compare the current and the forecasted performance of the project to the performance which was planned during the planning phase. This comparison can tell you whether the project's performance is on track or not. Hence, it can help you answer whether your planned scope, the costs you estimated, and your schedule is on track.

Perform Integrated Change Control Process

(*Please note that there is also a separate topic on how to make changes on a project which covers the entire process in much more detail. In this section, I will summarize it more briefly.)

Next is the perform integrated change control process. However, first we need to learn about what exactly is a change request. When you're working on any project whether it's a construction related project or a technology related project there are bound to be several changes which will happen during the course of the project. As the project manager, it is your responsibility to manage the changes that happen on a project.

Change requests refer to a formal request for changes or adjustments which need to be made on the project. Changes can be started by your customer, by your team members, or by yourself in case you notice the project requires them. The Perform integrated change control process is the formal process where change requests are evaluated and then they will be either accepted or rejected. It is not necessary for you to accept every change request that comes through. For any change request that you receive you need to evaluate them for the impact that they can have on the project. The impact of a change request needs to be evaluated on areas including:

- Cost
- Schedule
- Quality
- Risk
- Resources
- Customer Satisfaction

For example, you need to consider what will the effect of the cost on my project if the change request is implemented. Are my costs going to increase? Is the project going to take more time to complete? Is it going to decrease or increase the quality? Are there any risks of implementing that change request? Hence, you must consider multiple aspects before you actually implement a change request and accepted.

Close Project Process

This is the process in which you will complete and wrap up that project. Now let's talk about what does the project manager have to do to close the project. Firstly, it is very important that you make sure the work has been done according to the requirements of the project.

Secondly, you must get the formal acceptance of the project or the product from the customer. The formal acceptance means you show the final deliverable to the customer and see whether they accept it or not. At this point, if the customer accepts, this means the deliverable has been officially finalized and acknowledged by the customer.

Also,It is important to complete the financial reporting on the project and to complete the closure of the procurements on the purchases which you have made. You will collect and archive the project records and the knowledge created from the project so that they may be used for reference in future projects. You will also gather and update the final lessons which you learn. You will also deliver the completed product to the customer. This is different from getting the formal acceptance from the customer because in the first case you're getting the acknowledgement from the customer that they accept this product. After that, you also need to make sure that you're delivering the completed product to the customer for the final handoff. And finally, you will get feedback from the customer regarding the project.

Note that every project is closed, regardless of whether it is completed, or even if it is left incomplete and halted due to some reason, you must wrap up and close the project down officially.

Scope Management

What is Scope Management

The first important thing for us to know is, what does scope mean when it comes to project management?

Simply speaking, Scope refers to the work that is required to be done on the project.

Now let's talk about what is the purpose of the Scope Management.

Scope Management is all about ensuring that the work done on the project includes only the work required to complete the project and then making sure only that work is done and nothing extra is done on the project.

Therefore, we can say that Scope Management basically involves two things:

- Firstly, figuring out what sort of work is required to be done on the project.
- and Secondly, ensuring only the work required is executed on the project.

Understanding Scope Further

First, we'll understand how scope is developed on the project

At the beginning of the project all the requirements are collected from all the stakeholders who are involved on the project. These requirements are then prioritized as per the business case and the project requirements.

The Prioritization of requirements leads to determining what work is included in the project and what work is not included in the project i.e. to determine what is within scope and what is out of scope.

The scope is then approved formally before the work starts. By approved formally we mean to say you make it clear to everyone working on the project as to what work is needed to be done to complete the project. After that, you get a sign off to get their acknowledgement/buy in.

The scope of work is then represented by a WBS (Work Breakdown Structure). You can think of it as a detailed map of the project work or an overview of all the work to be done on the project. This greatly helps clarify the scope involved of the project.

Important notes you should know about managing scope:

Changes to scope are not readily allowed and can only be made with an approved change request. (This is because you set a scope baseline during planning, and the project is expected to follow this baseline throughout its duration. Therefore, changing any baseline should be considered a last resort option.)

Secondly, we should remember that Changes to scope are first analysed for their effect on project constraints, which include costs, time, risk, resources, customer satisfaction and quality.

Another thing to note is that Determining what is included and what is not included in the scope should be a continuous process by the Project Manager. This helps sure the project stays on course.

And finally, Changes to scope that do not fit with the Project Charter should not be approved.

Scope Management involves the following processes:
- Plan Scope Management
- Collect Requirements
- Define Scope
- Create WBS
- Validate Scope
- Control Scope

What are Project Requirements

Project requirements refer to the description and features of the product or service being developed. The actual requirements of a project consist of the detailed scope, i.e., the details of the work to be done on the project. Requirements are collected at a High Level in the Project Charter at the beginning of a project, these are then fleshed out to develop the detailed scope.

What are Constraints

A Constraint is any factor that limits your ability or your choices of doing the project.

An easy explanation would be to think of constraints as the variables or the things that can stop you from doing the project.

Constraints are identified during project initiating at a high level. Then, During Project Planning, constraints are detailed in the Define Scope Process. This means that constraints are identified from the top during the initiating stage, but it isn't until the define scope process that constraints are elaborated in detail and more information is collected and understood about them.

Let's look at the types of constraints a project can have, these include

- Schedule/Time
- Cost/Budget
- Risk
- Quality
- Scope
- Resources
- Customer satisfaction

Now let's understand how constraints can hold your project back from being done properly.

Let's consider the constraints of time and cost. E.g. If you have a schedule deadline for a project that is very near, it might limit your option for producing a high-quality product because you simply may not have the time to make it according to level of quality you want. Similarly, if you are being restricted by your cost and budget, you may not be able to include some features into a product because the project does not have the money to spare.

Analyzing the impact of constraints on a project

Firstly, note that is the project managers responsibility to identify and evaluate the effect of constraints. Secondly, Constraints can have an effect or impact on each other.

For example, if you're decreasing the amount of time taken to complete a project, you need to figure out if you'll be able to deliver the overall scope and requirements of the project. Similarly, by decreasing the cost or budget, you may put the project in jeopardy as customer satisfaction might decrease if you are unable to deliver the right quality.

Now let's talk about the Impact of project changes on Constraints. It is very important for the Project Manager to analyze the effect that changes on the project can have on constraints. In situations where changes are requested by clients, you need to analyze what impact the changes will have on any one of these constraints. For example, will a change on your software project, like the addition of a new feature, increase your cost and schedule for developing the software?

The impact of changes and constraints on a project needs to be monitored throughout the project so just remember that every action on a project might have consequences on its performance.

Product Scope and Project Scope

Product Scope

Product scope includes the **product** or **deliverable** of the project, it's features, and its functions. So when you define the product scope in the case of a software application, it will include information such as: What is the app all about, what features and functions does it have, and what will its design look like.

Project Scope

The **project scope** includes all the **work** that will go into creating and delivering the product of the project.

While product scope is concerned with what the product will look like and what will be its functions, on the other hand, the project scope includes project management activities such as meetings, developing reports, as well as planning and coordinating the project in order to achieve the product scope.

Hence, the work you will do to create the product, is known as project scope.

Gold Plating

Have you ever been in a situation where you tried to go the extra mile for the customer? You went above and beyond and did more work than what was required just to make sure the customer is satisfied?

Gold Plating refers to giving customers extra things on the project which are beyond the agreed scope. Examples can include developing more features on the product (e.g. including more features on the app), Delivering superior quality than what was required (using better material for building construction than what was initially agreed on etc.)

Well when it comes to project management, such a practice is not recommended. Sometimes, you may go above and beyond to provide customers with extras. However, we should note that this is a bad practice because

- Firstly, the customer has not asked for it
- Secondly, It increases your costs, schedule, and scope

At times, you might end up getting so hung up on going that extra mile, that you end up risking the main core requirement of the customer. No matter how many extras you give to the customer, if the customers main requirement is not addressed, your project has failed to deliver.

So what should be done instead, is that the teams effort should focus on fulfilling the existing requirements instead of going above and beyond to provide extras to the customer. This should be the priority, you do that one thing that was required, and you do it well, this is what is most important.

What are Baselines

Baselines are the approved versions of the scope, cost and schedule on a project. They are developed while Planning the project.

The project management plan includes 3 baselines: 1. Scope 2. Cost 3. Schedule. Together, the three are called the performance measurement baseline

In order to see whether the project is going well or not, the project performance is compared against the baselines to evaluate if the project is on track with the planned scope, schedule and cost.

For the project manager to be successful, the project must be followed according to the baselines, since these are your benchmarks against which you measure project performance.

What happens in case there are deviations from the baseline?

As the project goes on, the project manager monitors the performance of the project to see if there are any deviations from the performance measurement baseline.

In case there are any deviations from the baselines, change requests are submitted to bring the project performance back on track. Therefore, you cannot just directly implement changes on the project, you need to submit change requests officially.

Some of the major reasons for deviations from the baseline can include incomplete risk identification and inadequate risk management on the project. This makes sense since let's say if you didn't account for a major risk at the beginning of the project, and then it ends up effecting your project negatively later, that means it would derail the project's performance.

To summarize quickly, the project contains 3 baselines which include the

- the Scope Baseline
- the Schedule Baseline
- and Cost Baseline

All three combined are known as the performance measurement baseline

Performance Measurement Baseline = Scope Baseline + Schedule Baseline + Cost Baseline

Now, let's learn about the individual baselines one by one.

Scope Baseline:

The scope baseline contains the work to be done on the project. It includes documents such as

1. The Project Scope Statement
2. The Work Breakdown Structure (WBS)
3. and The WBS Dictionary

Schedule Baseline:

The schedule baseline contains the schedule and timelines the project is supposed to follow, this also includes the dates for starting and ending of each activity on the project. For every single important task that needs to be done to complete the project, you need to have a date for when it starts and when does it end. This will helpful in coming up with the timeline of the project and it enables you to evaluate how the project is progressing.

Cost Baseline:

The cost baseline refers to the money that has been approved for use on the project. The cost baseline is Time sensitive (which means it contains information regarding at what point in time will funds be required on the project).

What is a WBS (Work Breakdown Structure)

A WBS is a hierarchical structure which shows the total scope of work to be done on the project to create the deliverables. It shows all the deliverables of the project which are broken down into further smaller deliverables down to the lowest level of the project.

Having a WBS is beneficial since it gives you clarity on all the pieces of the project. It shows what are the individual smaller deliverables that are needed to create the bigger deliverables. This makes it easy to see how the deliverables are related to one another in the entire project. The project team finds it easy to see who is responsible for each of the different parts of the project and decreases ambiguity.

A WBS breaks down the deliverables into smaller pieces. Each deliverable is broken down until work packages are reached. Work packages are the items at the lowest level of the hierarchy in a WBS. As we move from the top to the bottom levels of the WBS, the project work is broken down in increasing detail.

The WBS is created by the entire project team because everyone who's work is involved in creating deliverables should create their own work package since they know their own work best. That is why the WBS is created with the help of the project team and stakeholders.

The WBS contains only those deliverables that are a part of the project and does not contain deliverables that are not included in the project. Hence, anything that is not a part of the WBS, is not a part of the project scope at that point in time.

Please note that while the WBS shows all the deliverables in a project,however, it does not show the actual tasks or work involved to produce the deliverables. This is because the actual task or work to produce a deliverable is known as an activity. We will define activities during schedule management. This is because once you know what you want to make, only then will you start to figure out what type of work would be required to make that product.

Lastly, to summarize it all and make it easy to understand, we can say that A WBS shows Scope in the form of deliverables.

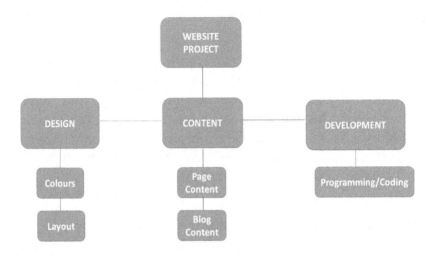

Now let's look at an of a sample WBS.

Example - Website Project:

- Final Deliverable: The Website
- Sub Deliverables: Design, Content, Development
- Work Packages: The work contained within each sub deliverable e.g. colors, page content, programming etc.

If you're developing a Web site, you need to look at what are the different things you need to do in order to develop the website. As you can see in the diagram above, the entire project work involved in developing the website has been broken down into smaller and more manageable components.

In this case we've broken down the work to be done on the project into three main categories. These include the design, content and the development of the Web site. These are the sub deliverables.

The end deliverable/outcome of the project is the website itself. We can see that the upper levels of the WBS contain the bigger parts of the project and these are then broken down into smaller pieces as the levels go downwards. Then, these three major categories have been broken down further into even more smaller components, which are the sub deliverables. These sub deliverables are then broken down further into work packages.

In order to develop the design for the website you need to come up with what sort of colors need to go on the site pages. You also need to know what the design of the layout of the different pages will be. Also, when it comes to the content of the Web site, you need to know what sort of content will go on to the different Web site pages and what sort of content will go on to the blog. Finally, when it comes to development, you need to make sure that you're programming and coding the website including any special functionalities it may require.

Work Packages:

The smallest and lowest pieces of a WBS are known as work packages. E.g. in this case, the colors and the layout would be the work packages that need to be done in order to prepare the design deliverable for the website. In simple terms, work packages are the things you need to make the deliverable above it. As you can see, the WBS makes it easy for you to estimate what will be the cost, time and resources required for doing different tasks.

For example, when it comes to the design, how much time and money will be required in order to complete the layout of the pages of the website. Similarly, when it comes to the development, what will be the cost, how many resources will be required and how much time will we need in order to get the programming and coding done on the website.

Furthermore, risks are evaluated on the basis on work packages, i.e. what are the risks involved in the getting the application code made for your software?

Hence, the WBS makes it easy for you to see all the scope of work which is involved in doing the project.

Next, let's learn about what is the WBS Dictionary.

WBS Dictionary:

The WBS dictionary contains the description and detailed information of every work package/deliverable. For example, when it comes to the Work Package of Software Code, or even Car Paint, it's entry in the WBS dictionary would contain:

- Description of the work package
- The Actual work involved to produce the work package
- The Resources involved in producing the work package
- Schedule
- The Cost
- The Interdependencies
- The Risks
- Quality metrics
- The Acceptance Criteria

How to Perform Scope Management

Plan Scope Management Process

Now that you've understood what Scope is, we're going to go over what are the different scope management processes. The first process is plan scope management and this is the process which will tell you about how to plan, execute and control scope on the project. As part of this process, you will develop what is known as the scope management plan and this is the most important deliverable of this process.

For the sake of simplicity and easy understanding, I'm going to use the following example: I'd like you to imagine a crowded marketplace with several shops and buildings, for example, think of Times Square in New York. As you can imagine, there would be a whole variety of different buildings, advertising, signboards, and other displays.

Think about it this way, what if you had to make a place like this. What if have you had to make all these different buildings and these displays. So, think about the variety of the different items that you would find in a crowded marketplace area and consider it as the scope of work that you have to do in order to complete the project, meaning the final deliverable would be that marketplace and all that it contains.

To pull this off, you need to create a plan which is going to detail about the work you need to do to create these different items. The scope management plan is your approach for managing scope on the project. This plan will detail about how you will fulfil the scope of the project, what methods and tools you will use, and how will you manage the control the scope.

Collect Requirements Process

How to Collect requirements

1. Identify all the stakeholders
2. Ask them for the requirements in detail

3. Rank the Requirements according to priority

Next is the Collect requirements process. In order to start off with any sort of a project you first need to collect the requirements for the project. It is also important to note that the requirements will mainly be collected from all the different stakeholders on the project. These requirements will form the basis for your project scope and furthermore, meaning they will be the basis of the work which has to be done on the project in order to make it successful.

For example, if you are a car manufacturer and you are developing a new type of car for your customers. Firstly, you would go around collecting all the requirements of your customers and then develop a car according to those requirements. You would not only consider your customers, but also other stakeholders such as the government and legal institutions. This is because you need to develop a product that can operate within the guidelines of traffic laws. Hence, your requirements from the customers and other stakeholders will form the basis for your project and the work which you need to do in order to develop the car which they require.

So how exactly do you collect requirements. Firstly, you will identify all the different stakeholders, and then, you need to ask them for their requirements in detail. For example, some of your customers might have requirements for the speed of the car, so that will give you more information about what sort of an engine do you need to implement it.

Some stakeholders might give you more information regarding their requirements for luxury or comfort. So that is how you will go about creating the scope for the type and material of seats that need to be installed. Once you have all those requirements you will then rank the requirements according to priority. The requirements of the most important stakeholders need to be fulfilled on a priority basis so keep those at the top of your checklist.

Next, let's quickly learn about what techniques you can use to collect requirements. One of the most effective methods, are personal interviews. You can ask people face to face or on a one on one basis as to what are their requirements. Also, you may conduct focus groups with a group of multiple stakeholders. You can also look at user stories. User stories are actual stories from the people who will actually end up using that product. Finally, you may consider benchmarking. You can evaluate a product in the market which is similar to yours and evaluate it. For example, for the car project that we're considering, you may search if there are other companies which have developed a similar type of car you can evaluate. You could benchmark what are the features of that car and what do you need to do to create it.

Once you have all the requirements, they are going to be compiled in a document which is known as the requirements documentation and this is the document which contains the actual acceptance criteria for the project. The acceptance criteria refer to all those things that you need to do in order to get that product accepted and approved.

Define Scope Process

After collecting requirements is the define school process. In this process, you will develop a more detailed description of the project and the product. It includes information such as:

- What exactly needs to be done on the project
- What are its deliverables.
- What is included in the Project
- What is NOT included on the project

Note: As a project manager, you need to be very specific in making sure that only the most relevant and required work is being done on the project. That is why it is also important to consider what is Not included in the project so that you have a very clear idea about the projects boundaries.

After having compiled all the requirements and once you have defined the scope, you will then be able to determine a budget and schedule for the project.

Furthermore, please remember that it is your top responsibility as a project manager to make sure that you develop a realistic budget and a realistic schedule that can actually achieve your scope without having any conflicts, delays or problems. Because it is only after you know what exactly needs to be done on the project that you will be able to tell how much time those tasks are going to take and how much money is it going to cost to do the project.

Create Work Breakdown Structure Process (WBS) Process

Now that you know all the work that needs to be done on the project it is time to place it in order. This is where you will take the work involved in doing the project and put it into an organized structure. This structure is known as a WBS, Work breakdown Structure. The WBS is a hierarchy-based structure which shows you the overall scope of work which needs to be done on the project in order to create the final deliverable. For example, if you were to build a car, the WBS would list Car as a final deliverable, and below it, it would have its component deliverables, including: Engine, Wheels, Doors, Paint etc.

To keep it simple, think of it as a chart which details all the work that needs to be done on the project in the form of actual deliverables, NOT the actions involved in creating those deliverables. E.g. the WBS would list car paint but not the action of painting.

The WBS helps you see the work more conveniently and easily because it breaks down all the deliverables and the project work by decomposing it into smaller and more manageable components. Because the work is broken down into smaller pieces, it makes it easier to estimate the cost, time and resources which are required for the individual components.

Validate Scope Process

Next is the Validate Scope process. As you're getting work done on the project, it is important to have continuous meetings with the customer/sponsor of the project. These meetings are held to obtain formal acceptance of the deliverables of the project. This helps in making sure that whatever work you are getting done on the project and the final deliverables you are creating, are in line with the requirements of the customer and the sponsor. You don't want to be in a situation where you create the deliverables and then at the end of the day your customer rejects what you worked hard to make.

By having frequent meetings, you can get the customers go ahead. While you are having the review for the validate scope process, the customer will either accept the deliverables or they can also request you for any changes that they want to make on the deliverables you are creating.

Control Scope Process

Lastly, controlling scope is mainly concerned with measuring and analysing the work performance against the scope baseline. You're checking and measuring as to whether the work that you're doing is in sync with your baseline. Only the work required to fulfil the requirements of the project should be carried out, anything else is extraneous and unnecessary, so that is what you're protecting the project against at this point.

At this point, you're also managing the scope changes in case the customer has requested for any additions or modifications to the project.

Schedule Management

What is Schedule Management

Schedule management involves the development of the project schedule, or rather, the timeline which the project is supposed to follow. It involves planning the work required to complete the project in a way that all of the different requirements are completed in a timely manner, as per the deadlines.

It also includes how activities will be prioritized and how will the activities be sequenced so that the work is done in the right order.

The most important output of Schedule Management is the Project Schedule. The project work is supposed to follow the project schedule properly to successfully complete the project. Project Schedules are developed to ensure that projects are completed within a specific time frame as decided by the project manager. The schedule keeps track of and helps you evaluate progress on the project. Most projects will have milestones on them. These milestones can be considered as checkpoints to evaluate the amount of progress you have made.

As a project manager, you are ultimately responsible for the Project Schedule. The development of a realistic project timeline and duration depends on your acumen and analysis of the dynamics and people surrounding the project. That is why it is important to consider all the factors surrounding the project before you start executing it. The bottom line is, you need to have a realistic schedule, stay away from unrealistic scenarios where you commit to getting the work done much earlier or much later than what it would actually take to complete the work.

When developing the schedule, here are some areas to consider that will help ensuring your estimates are as realistic as possible:

- How much time would your team members take to complete each task?

- What is their skill level, how fast can they get the work done?
- Will your suppliers be able to provide you with raw materials on time?
- What are the possible things that can go wrong with the project and how much time do you estimate those setbacks can cost you in terms of hours/days/months?

These are just some of the things you can ask yourself before you develop a project schedule.

Next, here are all the Schedule Management Processes we will discuss ahead:

- Plan Schedule Management
- Define Activities
- Sequence Activities
- Estimate Activity Durations
- Develop Schedule
- Control Schedule

How to Perform Schedule Management

Plan Schedule Management Process

Schedule management is all about how you're supposed to manage time on the project. Plan schedule management involves planning, managing, and controlling the schedule for your project. It is your responsibility as a project manager to manage the time which is taken to do the work on the project.

We're going to use a simplified example of constructing a house to facilitate ease of understanding. The diagram below shows the project schedule network diagram, and this is what you will use in order to manage time on the project. Think about all the things you need to do in order to construct a building or a house. So first you will select the design of the house. Then, you will purchase the materials to build it. Then, you will construct the ground floor, followed by constructing the roof to top it all off. Finally, you will have the house completed.

Schedule Network Diagram

Define Activities Process

Let's learn about what is the define the activities process. First, let's learn about what exactly are activities?

Activities are the tasks or actions which are required to produce deliverables, it is the actual work which goes into making a product. If you want to make a new home, the first thing you would need to do in terms of work would be to select a design of the house. This is the actual work that you're doing, i.e. going through a selection process.

On the other hand, the deliverable will be the shortlisted designs of the House or the blueprints for the design that you've selected. Therefore, Activities are the actions, whereas the deliverable is the final completed output. Activities are important because they can be used as a basis for estimating, scheduling, executing monitoring and controlling the product work.

In the diagram, you will see all the different activities which are involved in constructing the house. Note that this is the work involved in getting the house made. You need to select the house design, you need to purchase the materials which are required to construct it, you need to construct the ground floor, and finally You need to construct the roof. Finally, you can complete the house.

Activities are used as a basis because if you know what kind of work you need to do to complete the house then you can estimate what will be the costs for it. You can also estimate what will be the time required to do that specific activity. So that is why we say that activities can be used as a basis.

Difference between Work Packages and Activities:

Let's quickly clarify the difference between these two concepts to make sure you fully understand.

On a project, work is divided into:

- Work packages – The actual deliverables produced on the project
- Activities – The actual actions required to produce those deliverables
- Example of Deliverables: House Design/Blueprints
- Example of an Activity: Selection of House Design

Sequence Activities Process

Next let's learn about what is the sequence activities process. So now that you have defined what exactly are the activities, now it is important to sequence the activities. The sequence activities process involves putting the activities in a sequence. So simply speaking, you're putting all the work required to do the project in a certain order, i.e., you're organizing activities in the order in which the work will be done.

For example, you can't really construct the roof of the house unless you've constructed the ground floor. Similarly, you can't construct the ground floor unless you have the materials for it. So in this process, you will order the activities in the way that the work is supposed to be done.

Estimate Activities Process

After putting the activities in the sequence, it is important to estimate how much time will each of those activities take. Hence, the estimate activity durations process estimates the amount of time it will take the resources to complete the activities (By resources, we are referring to both the material resources and the human resources being used on the project).

For example, how much time would it take the construction workers to construct the ground floor, and if you're using construction machinery, how much time will it take specific machines to produce specific deliverables for the house. As you can see from the diagram, it is going to take two days for you to select and shortlist the design of the house and it will take you another two days after that to purchase the materials. It will take three days to construct the ground floor and five days to construct the roof.

Depending on the nature of your project whether it is a tech related project or a construction related project, you need to first define what exactly is the work that needs to be done in order to complete this project. Then, sequence the work in order, and finally, you need to see how much time that specific work is going to take. You need to do this for all the activities involved on the project to come up with a realistic schedule estimate.

Develop Schedule Process

Now that you have all the information related to the work that you need to do in order to complete the project, it is now time to develop a schedule. The develop schedule process is the one in which the finalized and approved date for the project is created.

As the project manager, you will analyse the schedule activities, the activity durations, the resource requirements and the schedule constraints in order to develop the schedule. You will use this information to develop the schedule model that will serve as the baseline for the schedule of the project.

The schedule model contains the final planned dates for completing the activities which are required to do the project.

Now let's see how the product manager can develop a schedule. The schedule is represented by the schedule network diagram and it shows the details about what the schedule for your project is going to look like.

So firstly, the schedule network diagram contains an overview which shows you all of the work and activities which are required to do the project.

Secondly, it also shows you the order in which the work is supposed to be done on the project. Finally, the diagram also shows the durations, or the time required for each of the activities to be done.

So once you have collected:

- Information on the activities required to complete the project
- The order in which they are supposed to occur

- The durations or time which they're going to take

You can then complete the entire schedule network diagram.

Control Schedule Process

Lastly, we have the control schedule process. This is the process in which you will monitor the project's activities and you will manage changes to the schedule baseline.

You need to ensure that the planned dates and timelines in the schedule are being followed as close to the plan as possible while the project is being executed. Avoid any sort of delays on the project since delays cost time and money.

Finally, the control schedule process also involves taking corrective and preventive actions in order to keep the product in line with the original plan. In case you notice that something is going wrong with the schedule or if any activities are being delayed and they're keeping you from reaching the project deadline, ensure that you're taking the right corrective and preventive measures so that you can achieve your projects goal and complete it on time. Corrective measures refer to those actions which bring your projects schedule performance back on track while preventive measures refer to taking care of potential problems in advance so that they do not occur on the project in the first place.

Cost Management

What is Cost Management

Every Project costs money and has a budget allocated to it. Your victory is in ensuring that the Project Costs remain less than the Project Budget.

Every resource used, no. of hours worked, materials consumed, these are just some of the aspects that can have a monetary value attached to them. In the worst-case scenario, they can end up costing way more than the budget that was initially planned. A successful project manager manages the costs of the project in a way that keeps the expenditure within the budget and still delivers it on time.

Cost Management includes determining all the different types of costs on the project and coming up with a budget the project is supposed to follow. This process involves activities that ensure that the project is completed within the budget that has been approved for it and that the project does not end up overspending the budget.

It also involves knowing the costs of the human and material resources required for project completion. This is important because the project manager needs to have all relevant the relevant and correctly measured costs in order to determine a budget in which the project and its objectives can be successfully completed.

There are a lot of things that can go wrong in projects. It is highly recommended that you allocate a certain amount of money as a buffer to handle those mishaps. This amount for these emergency scenarios should be included within the budget you will create for the project. This practice will do you wonders and save you a lot of hassle.

Cost Management involves the following processes:

- Plan Cost Management
- Estimate Costs
- Determine Budget
- and Control Costs

How to Perform Cost Management

Plan Cost Management Process

This is the process in which you're going to develop all the guidelines on how you're going to manage and control costs on the project. This includes taking certain strategic level decisions when it comes to the project. For example, if you're working on a construction project you need to determine, are you going to purchase the machinery which you require on the project or is it a better idea to rent it or to lease it.

Another important decision to make is how are you going to finance the project. Are you going to use the organization's own money and its own capital, or is it a better idea to finance the project by taking loans or debt?

Estimate Costs Process

Next is the estimate costs process and this is where you're going to figure out what would it cost and how much money/capital is required in order to complete the project. To do this, estimate all the costs for each of the different activities that you're going to do on the project. So for example, if you're working on developing a website project, you would estimate the costs for all of its different activities which includes designing the website, all the way to coding/programming and then conducting quality assurance.

Hence, you need to evaluate how much is it going to cost to do each of those different actions or activities in order to complete the project. Hence, this is how you will estimate costs when it comes to projects, by individually gauging how each item/activity will cost.

Note that it is important to estimate costs for a variety of different areas in order to come up with the project budget. The budget would include costs of:

- Materials and Supplies (Wood, Steel, Cement etc.)

- Salaries of Employees, Project Team and Labour Costs
- Equipment and machinery (Cranes, Transport Vehicles)
- Training for the employees (Safety Training, Communication Skills, Teamwork)
- Implementing Quality Measures on the project-Costs involved in making sure the product has been developed as per requirements, i.e. Costs for doing checks and balances.
- Risk – It is important to include the costs of managing and handling the risk within the project budget from the beginning.
- Fixed Costs – E.g. Rent

Once you've come up with the costs of all the activities you can then combine all of those to come up with the project budget.

Determine Budget Process

Next, we're going to talk about the determine budget process. The budget is developed by adding up the individual costs of all the activities which are involved in doing the project. I will reiterate this another way just to make sure you completely understand: the individual costs of activities are added to develop the budget for the project.

It is also important to note that the budget contains the time-based funding requirements. This means that the budget covers whatever costs will be incurred at whatever point in time they will be incurred on the project. This is because at different points of the project you can have different costs. Knowing at which point is the project going to cost you more and at which point is it going to cost lesser can help you in making better decisions when it comes to managing costs.

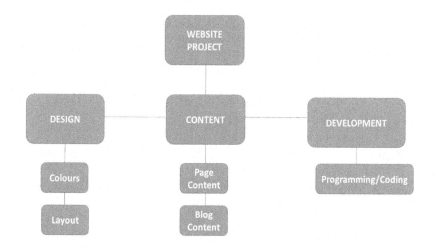

Example:

Let us continue our example of making a website to make it easy to understand how to determine the budget.

As you may remember, the WBS shows the project in terms of deliverables, and the lowest level of the WBS are known as work packages. Note that Design is a major deliverable required to make the website. Colours and Layouts are work packages which are required to make the Design deliverable.

Now, note that activities are the actual work that is done to create a deliverable. Here is an example of an activity and in parallel, an example of the deliverable it creates.

Deliverable: Site Layout

Activity: Create Site Layout

Now we are going to roll up the cost of the activities into the work package, and then in turn, roll it up into the cost of the deliverable known as Website Design.

Activity Costs for Website Design

1. Create site layout - $500
2. Develop colour schemes - $200

3. Insert Pictures for webpages - $100 (this item isn't in the diagram but I've added it here just for your understanding.)

Cost of Website Design = Cost of all the activities involved in Website Design

Hence,

Cost of Website Design = Create Site layout + Develop Colour Schemes + Insert Pictures for webpages

Cost of Website Design = $500 + $200 + $100 = $800

Next, we are left with the calculation of the deliverables Content and Development.

You will follow the same process for the calculation of their costs i.e., by calculating the totals costs of the activities involved in creating those deliverables.

So for example, for Content, you will add the costs for:

Cost of Website Content = Create Page Content + Create Blog Content

Final Budget for Website = Design + Content + Development (Sum of all the activities involved in creating these deliverables)

Hence, the budget for creating the website will be the sum of all the activities involved in creating the deliverables on the project, plus Contingency reserves. Contingency reserves refer to the money reserves allocated to take care of risks.

There are other components to the project budget, however, we will not be delving into complications since this material is meant to quickly prepare you to dive headfirst into project management by getting the fundamentals right.

Control Costs Process

Lastly, we have the control costs process. This is where you will monitor and measure the costs on the project.

The most important thing to make sure of in this process is that the project costs do not exceed the funds which are available for the project. It should be your priority as a project manager to make sure that the project is being done within the budget that you have allocated for it.

Furthermore, it's also important that you're monitoring the work performance against the money which is being spent in order to get that work done.

For example, if you spent a hundred dollars on the project, you need to evaluate whether you have gotten your money's worth. Does the work that has been done on the project justify the $10,000 that you spent on it? This is helpful in evaluating whether the project is on track or not.

Performing Cost Management is a very important responsibility for all project managers, they have to be estimated correctly at the beginning and then monitored constantly to ensure the project is completed within budget.

Quality Management

What is Quality Management

What is Quality?

Before we talk about Quality Management, it is important know what exactly does quality mean in the context of a project. Simply put, Quality is the extent to which a project satisfies the requirements of the customer.

Quality cannot be achieved unless you have collected and fulfilled all the requirements of the project. Therefore, it is vital to collect the project's requirements in significant depth. Because if you do not have the requirements in detail, how would you fulfill them, and as a result achieve quality?

Hence, you need to collect as much information as you can regarding the project's requirements. The more detailed your requirements gathering effort is, the greater the extent to which you can fulfill them, and the greater the level of quality you can achieve on your project.

Quality Management.

Quality Management involves the processes and activities that ensure that the project and product requirements are validated, checked and fulfilled. So it's all about making sure the project is going smoothly and that you're producing the correct product as per what your customer wanted, using the right processes. Hence, this process also involves the creation of policies and procedures that need to be followed during the project to ensure that the project meets the needs required by the customer. Therefore, the focus is not only on ensuring the creation of right products, but also on having the correct processes.

One of the major goals of Quality management is to prevent deviations from the project requirements and to ensure that the requirements of the project have been fulfilled in a correct manner.

To achieve this, the processes and procedures help in keeping a check on ensuring the project work is on the right track. These processes must be followed and implemented while the project work is actually being done and carried out.

Quality Management includes the following processes:

- Plan Quality Management
- Perform Quality Assurance
- and Control Quality

How to Ensure Quality on a project

While working on projects, there are expectations for products to perform according to a specified criterion. For example, when you buy a super car like Ferrari, you would expect it to travel fast at a certain speed. If you were the engineer, how you ensure that the car you're producing meets those requirements?

Here's how:

- The first step is to Define what is an acceptable level of quality on the project.
- Then, determine what metrics will be used to measure quality before actual work on the project begins.
- After that, Inspect and check the work as it is done on the project,
- Then, Check the quality of activities and work packages before they are completed.

Putting it simply:

- We are determining what is the desired level of performance in the product
- And then Measuring the actual performance against the quality metrics that we have defined.

By following these points, we can ensure that the deliverable or product that is being created, fulfills our standards and benchmarks and most importantly, fulfills the projects requirements.

Prevent Problems instead of Dealing with them

Always prioritize preventing problems from occurring on the project in the first place, instead of having to find them and deal with them later. Avoid solving problems during the project execution stage, meaning while the actual work on the project is going on. Instead, your focus should be on preventing problems as opposed to dealing with them. Therefore, it is always better to plan quality beforehand as opposed to inspecting problems during the project.

Quality must be part of how you plan the project, so it needs to be planned into the project from the beginning and not kept as a separate task to be taken care of later. By planning quality into the project, you can help avoid a lot of problems as the project progresses.

How to Perform Quality Management

To develop a successful product, it is important to adhere to quality measures on the project. The Project Manager is ultimately responsible that quality standards are exercised on the project.

Plan Quality Management Process

Now first let's learn about what is the Plan Quality Management process. As a project manager, you will identify all the requirements and the existing standards of quality in the industry that you're operating in.

Whether you're developing software applications or automobiles, it is important to know what the quality standards of that industry are so that you can produce products that adhere to certain quality standards.

Secondly, it is vital to identify all the customer's requirements and standards. It is important to make sure that the product that you're developing meets the customer's requirements as closely as possible.

Lastly, you need to create project specific standards so that you can measure the project's performance according to your own project's customised standards.

Manage Quality Process

Manage quality is performed to check whether the right processes and procedures are being followed on the project. It is important to note that the focus of this process is to ensure that the right processes and procedures are being used to develop the product on the project.

The emphasis here is not on the deliverables, instead, it is on checking whether the processes and procedures are actually being followed in the right way. E.g. Are you using the right standards to produce the latest model of the energy efficient car, are you using the right standards and procedures to create the latest version of your software application etc.

Control Quality Process

Once you've made sure that you're using the right procedures to create or develop the product, next is the control quality process.

The Control Quality Process is about ensuring that the deliverables meet the quality standards. The tool that's used in this case is inspection. The project manager is involved in examining and measuring a product or a deliverable to see whether it meets the requirements shared by the customer. It's about ensuring your product fulfils the criteria shared by your customer and the level of performance they are expecting from the final product.

Difference between Managing Quality and Controlling Quality

The distinction is that managing quality is like quality assurance, and it is more concerned with checking the actual process of producing the final deliverable and not the deliverable itself. Hence, the emphasis is on whether the right processes are being adhered to or not.

On the other hand, control quality is more concerned with checking the actual quality of the deliverable itself and whether it fulfils the quality standards as planned.

Another important distinction is that Control Quality is performed before you hand off the final product to the customer. Meaning an inspection of the product is carried out to check whether it meets all the industry standards/requirements and the customer's requirements. Then, finally you hand the finalized and completed deliverable of the project off to the customer.

Resource Management

What is Resource Management

Resource management is all about managing the people who are responsible for getting the project done (e.g. engineers, architects, consultants). It also includes managing the physical resources which are going to be used on the project. This includes things such as materials (e.g. steel, cement), equipment (e.g. safety helmets, construction tools) and the different types of machinery (e.g. cranes, vehicles).

Simply speaking, we can say that resource management includes both human resource management as well as physical resource management.

Now let's look at the various tasks which are involved in resource management:

Resource management includes how to involve people on the project. It also includes how do you go about identifying the different team members who will work on the project. You will also define the roles and responsibilities of the people who will be working on the project.

It comprises of ensuring the availability of the right type of material resources at the right time and the right place on the project. Furthermore, it includes creating reward systems for the team which is working on the project. Also, it comprises of improving the performance of different individuals and the teams working on the project.

Lastly, it also involves keeping track of the performance of the people who are working on the project. The Project team consists of the people who are responsible for completing the project, meaning doing the actual work on the project. The Project Management team is responsible for managing the project during initiating, planning, executing, monitoring, controlling, and closing the project. They help the project manager in taking care of the project management activities.

However, these two can differ across organizations. For example, in organizations which follow an Agile methodology, the project management team members may also be involved in doing the actual work on the project as well since they may be Generalists (People who can wear multiple hats and do different types of work rather than specialize in one specific area), hence, this is not a hard and fast rule, and it depends on your organizations structure.

Resource Management includes the following processes:

- Plan Resource Management
- Estimate Activity Resources
- Acquire Resources
- Develop Team
- Manage Team
- Control Resources

How to Perform Resource Management

Resources can be divided into the

- Human resources
- Material resources

The human resources involve skilled professionals that you would require to be a part of your project team. Secondly, it would also involve the material resources which would include things such as factory and construction machinery to be used on your project.

Now let's learn about how you're going to manage resources on a project:

Plan Resource Management Process

The first process is plan resource management. The first purpose of plan resource management is that it clarifies the responsibilities and the work for the project team and the stakeholders who are involved on the project. So as a project manager, it is your responsibility to provide clarity on the work the people are supposed to do on the Project.

Secondly, it also provides information on what are the different materials and the physical resources which will be used on the project. For example, if you're constructing a building, what are the different types of construction machinery that you need to use on your project. If you're working on an I.T. project, what type of machines or computers (what specifications) do you need to use and what type of software would you need to use on the project.

As far as human resources are concerned, you need to know what type of specific skill sets you require in order for your project to succeed. It is also important to note how will you go about acquiring those people and resources for your project.

You will also plan for staff acquisition, which shows your approach for where the project staff will come from (borrowing from another department, new hiring, freelancing etc) and at what point of the project will you procure the staff for the project. You may make use of Resource Calendars, which will contain information on when your resources will be available to work on the project and when will they be actively involved on the project in getting work done.

Lastly, you will also determine on how reporting relationships will be developed, and the levels of authority between your different resources, i.e., who answers to whom.

Estimate Activity Process

Next is the estimate activity resources process. Now that you have defined exactly what sort of activities will be performed in order to complete the project and then once you have sequenced those activities in terms of in which order does the work need to be done on the project, you then require two things in order to estimate the activity resources:

Firstly, you need to know exactly what type of resources will be needed to get the project done. What type of raw materials do you need to use and what type of equipment do you need. What type of specific machines do you require and what sort of professionals do you need to work on your project.

Secondly, it is important to determine is the quantity of the resources which will be needed to do the project. For example, if you're developing an application or a website, how many designers do you require, how many people do you require who have a programming and coding skillset etc.

If you're constructing a building, how many engineers do you require and how much labour do you need to complete the project. The benefit of determining the type and quantity of resources is that it allows you to create more accurate cost and duration estimates. E.g. if you know that you will require five engineers to work on constructing the building, then what will be their cost and for how much duration do you actually need them to work on the project.

And so estimating activity resources is all about determining the type of resources and then the quantity of those resources.

Acquire Resources Process

Next is the acquire resources process. Any project can involve hundreds of different types of resources and so it is important for the project manager to know how exactly you will go about acquiring those resources for your project.

So, when it comes to human resources, how will you acquire I.T. experts? Can you find such resources within your own company or in your own department? Or do you need to hire somebody from outside? Also, if you are constructing a building how will you go about acquiring the architects. Can you borrow these resources from within your organization or are you going to contract the design work outside to some company? Furthermore, when it comes to material resources and if you require construction machinery, then are you going to buy the construction machinery, is it already available, or are you going to rent it from some an external party?

You also need to consider how you are going to procure the raw materials for your project. It is also important to consider that resources can either be internal or external. So either your company will already have those assets, the raw materials and people with specific skill sets, or you might need to outsource the work.

Hence, as part of the acquire resources process, you need to determine what is the best way forward when it comes to acquiring those resources. As a part of this process you will be involved in several different things. Firstly, you need to confirm the availability of these resources, so you need to confirm whether that programming expert is available on the dates of your project or whether they're working on a separate project.

You might also need to negotiate for the best resources, so you might come across situations where you need to borrow some skilled professionals from a separate department. In this case, you would talk to their functional manager in order to borrow those resources for your project. You might also be involved in hiring new human resources specifically for your project. Also, you might be involved in outsourcing your product work by hiring external resources who do not necessarily belong to your organization. So for example you might hire freelancers in order to work on designing the user interface or coding your software project.

Develop Project Team Process

As a project manager, it is important to invest in the development of your project team to reap better performance, productivity, and wellbeing. Ensure that your team has high performance by constantly improving the skills, knowledge, teamwork and motivation levels. A team that is well taken care of can result in higher satisfaction and decreased turnover.

Team building activities can help since it is important for your team members to work well together. Take them for dinners or lunches or have them play sports together. Activities through which you can get the team to get to know each other better are healthy for the project team's bonding and mutual understanding.

Secondly, send your project team members for training in order to get them upgraded on the latest skills. Having an up to date skillset can ensure your team continues to deliver and can take on more challenging projects in the future. Third is colocation, this refers to having all the members of your project team in the same place and working on the project together. Colocation can help improve the performance of the team because it would allow for lesser information gaps and miscommunication since ambiguities can be clarified right there and then.

Lastly, are rewards and recognition. Bonus incentives may include monetary, off the job rewards or even on the job rewards such as trainings and working on preferred projects. Set KPI's and milestones and recognize project team member's for completing important project phases. Setting short achievable goals can keep team member's motivated and energized for the rest of the journey through the project's life.

Manage Project Team Process

Managing your project team involves the everyday management and progress tracking of the people who are working on the project.

Firstly, you need to track the performance of the project team. Then, based on the performance of the team members, you will share feedback with them. Also, you will resolve any issues within the team if there are any conflicts. Finally, in case there are any changes required on the project, you will implement them in order to make sure that you're optimizing and improving the team's performance.

Control Resources Process

Since you need to manage the physical resources and materials which are being used on the project, you are responsible for ensuring that the right resources tools and machinery are available:

- At the right time
- At the right place
- In the right quantity

Furthermore, it helps you evaluate how many physical resources were planned to be used on the project and how many did you actually end up using. So the control resources process can help you in monitoring the cost of the resources that you have used on the project and also keeps the project expenditure in check.

Communications Management

What is Communications Management

Communications are the most important role of a project manager.

This can be understood by the fact that up to **90 percent** of a project managers time can be spent communicating on a project.

Projects can be overwhelming. This is understandable since each large project contains numerous people working alongside one another. Each of these individuals may be busy in doing their own work, which is why there needs to be someone who has an overhead perspective on the project. Furthermore, this is also why the project manager is the core of a project who knows how to connect the pieces of the project's puzzle together.

Because a project manager is at the center of a project, it is important to ensure that information is flowing appropriately across the different people involved on the project.

You need to ensure that the right information reaches the right people at the right time and in the right format.

Therefore, it is necessary to create a communication management plan to manage communications between all involved stakeholders on the project.

The purpose of Communication Management on a project is to ensure that the right project information (whatever is most relevant for whom) is distributed to relevant stakeholders (Project team, Sponsor, Project team, Customer) in a timely and efficient way.

Communications Management involves the following processes:

- Plan Communication Management process
- Manage Communications process
- Control Communications process -

How to Perform Communications Management

Plan Communications Management

Communication management is the process in which you will determine the stakeholder information needs and you will then define a communication approach on how to address those information needs. The success of a project relies on the effectiveness of the information flow between different stakeholders. The project manager is responsible for organizing a smooth flow of relevant information across the project's participants and ensuring its convenient accessibility.

On any project, you will be dealing with a variety of different stakeholders, ranging from your project team, the customer, senior management and also the external stakeholders, like suppliers, vendors and partners

Each of these different stakeholders will have different communication requirements, therefore, the most important task, is to analyse the stakeholder's communication requirements. (What is their involvement on the project, what are their interests in the project)

Ask yourself the following before starting any project-

- What sort of communication do each of our stakeholders require? (What do we need to communicate to our senior management, project team, vendors, partners, freelancers, contractors etc)
- In what form do we need to share that information? (PowerPoint, Meetings, Presentations)
- How often should we share that information with them?
- When exactly should we share that information?

Let's explore these thoughts further:

For example, in the case of senior management, you would share the product milestones and the status of the product.

It is important to determine in what form will you be communicating the information to your different stakeholders. For instance, to share project progress with senior management, will you be delivering presentations in person or will you be emailing the status reports? How often and with which stakeholders will you have meetings?

Therefore, as a project manager, you will define an approach for communicating with each of the different stakeholders.

Communication management is also concerned with how you will store, maintain, distribute, and retrieve the information. Most importantly, you need to determine exactly what type of information will be communicated to which people.

It also needs to be decided what will be the format or the method in which that information will be communicated.

Also, determine how frequently will you share that information, is it going to be a weekly report, weekly meeting or is it going to be daily or monthly.

You also need to make sure that you're confirming that the information that you have shared has been received and understood.

Manage Communications Process

This is the actual process in which you will gather and provide information which is required by the stakeholders. Also, it is very important for you to make sure that the information that you sent has been received and understood. Therefore, make it a point to follow up with stakeholders to get to know whether they have actually understood the information that they've received.

I cannot stress how important this is and how much trouble this simple act can save you. See, when you confirm a person's acknowledgement, you have gained publicly provable buy-in from them. E.g. in a car manufacturing project, let's say you had an urgent conversation about your required specifications for engine parts with your parts supplier vendor. After your conversation, it is useful to send a follow up email mentioning your conversation and your product specifications, just to ensure you both are on the exact same page.

Furthermore, it can help you in developing a better relationship with the stakeholders and it can also help you in terms of solving problems. For example, the stakeholders might be able to share some feedback on how you can improve the performance of the project based on the information that you just shared with them.

Monitor Communications Process

This process is about ensuring that your communication management plan is being followed properly on the project.

Is the right kind of information being provided? Are the communication requirements of the stakeholders being fulfilled? Are people receiving the information at the right time? Does the project team have all the information they require to carry out the project? Is the senior management updated with project progress on a regular basis?

The goal of this process is to make sure the correct information reaches the right kind of people at the correct time when it is required.

Risk Management

What is Risk Management

What does Risk Mean?

First, let's understand what exactly Risk means in the context of project management. Risk is an uncertain event which may have a positive or negative effect on the project if it occurs. It can be in the form of opportunities, as well as threats. What we must understand is that risks can be both positive and negative, positive risks being in the form of opportunities and negative risks being in the form of threats.

Risks are identified throughout the project's life, firstly, at the beginning during project initiating, they are identified as the project charter is being developed. After that, as the project goes on, they are constantly updated as you come across new risks.

Once a risk is identified, it should be analysed and then, you need to plan responses on how to manage or handle that risk. These responses are known as risk response plans.

This brings us to the question -

How does a project manager handle risks on the project?

A project's line of Defence against risks include:

- Primary Risk Response Plans
- Contingency Plans

Let's try to understand the role of each of these plans

Risks are taken care of by risk response plans. These are plans which contain specific information on how to manage or handle the risk. They are the primary form of defence against identified risks and consist of the strategy for addressing risks before they occur. Most risks will be expected to be addressed by the primary risk response plans.

The advantage of a risk response plan is that in case a risk event occurs on the project, there are plans ready to deal with it. This means that since the risk was identified earlier, risk response plans were prepared to deal with the risk in case it actually occurs on the project.

Next, let's talk about contingency plans

Contingency plans are meant to tackle the remaining risks that are left over after the primary risk response plans have taken care of addressing risks on the project. These are responses for accepted risks which may become more significant in the future, or they may be used to address risks which were unable to be taken care of through the primary risk response plans.

Most importantly, we must understand that the real success for a project manager is to prevent problems instead of having to solve them because they occurred. Hence, the real success lies in not having to deal with problems in the first place. This is because dealing with problems means that you have allowed a certain problem to occur. Whereas the best thing for a project manager to do is to focus on not letting problems not been in the first place.

It is important to constantly review risks during meetings. The discussions should cover whether there have been any new risks and the status of the previous risks. Being proactive will help you keep your project safe from unforeseen damage if you make it a regular point of discussion.

Therefore, you need to be prepared beforehand for any risks that may occur on the project, and this can be done by proper risk management on a project.

What are the objectives of risk management on the project?

The objective is to increase the probability and impact of opportunities or positive risks.

Secondly, the objective is to Decrease the Probability and Impact of Threats or negative risks on the project.

Here are the Risk Management Processes:

- Plan Risk Management
- Identify Risks
- Perform Qualitative Analysis
- Perform Quantitative Analysis
- Plan Risk Responses

How to Perform Risk Management

Plan Risk Management Process

The first process is Plan Risk management, and this is where you will plan for dealing with risks on the project.

One of the most important outputs of this process is the risk management plan. This is a detailed plan for how you're going to tackle risk as it occurs on your project. The risk management plan includes information on several different areas, the first being methodology. Methodology covers the approaches the approaches and the processes that you will use in order to tackle the risk on the project.

Next are the rules and responsibilities. In order to tackle the risks, you need to define what will be the different responsibilities of the people in your team when it comes to risks. This involves defining specific risk owners.

Risk owners are those people who will manage or take care of the risk in case it occurs during the project's life. Risk owners can be any stakeholder, this could be somebody who is working on the project team or even one of your suppliers. So depending on the type of risk, you will designate different risk owners as to who would be the most appropriate person to take care of that risk.

Next is budgeting. You need to define how much money are you going to set aside to take care of the risks. Another aspect is timing, when exactly do you expect the risks to occur?

Then, we have risk categories. What are the different categories of risk that you expect to encounter on the project. E.g. Environmental risk, Market Risk, Financial Risk etc

Next, definitions of probability and impact. You need to know what are the different probabilities of the risks that can occur on the project and what kind of an impact or influence can they have on the project's performance. Probability would refer to the likelihood of that risk happening, while the impact would be measured in terms of its effect on the project e.g., impact could be gauged in terms of cost (profit or loss) or time (number of days).

To make it easy to compare risks between different projects, organizations create definitions of risk probability and impact. E.g., you would create a scale out of 10 for both Probability and Impact. A 4-impact rating for a risk could mean a loss of $40,000 for your organization. For another company, a 4-impact rating might mean a loss of $3000.

Finally, we need to consider Risk Tracking. This involves how will you track the risk across the duration of the project's life. It involves keeping a check on the likelihood of the risk occurring so that you can act accordingly.

Then we need to take stakeholder tolerance levels into account. You need to know the limits or the tolerances that the stakeholders have when it comes to encountering different risks on the project.

Next is reporting. In case a risk occurs on the project, how will you report it to the different stakeholders.

Identify Risks Process

Next is the identify risks process. The first thing note is that risk identification occurs throughout the life of the project. You constantly need to be on the lookout for risks as you're doing your project. Another aspect is that risks will be identified at a high level during the initiating stage and once identified, these will then be added to the project charter. Think of the most important risks which you can possibly occur on the project and note them down. You should prepare for them beforehand, so the earlier you are able to identify the most significant risks the better it is.

Then finally, the detailed risk identification will occur while you're planning the project. This is where the majority of the risks will be identified. There might be several risks which are involved in every process of the project, you can identify and make plans to handle them as you go along with the project. However, it is always advisable that you identify the most important risks as you are starting off with the product and to make your plan sufficiently detailed to handle risks earlier on.

It is not advisable to recognize and handle risks later in the project, you should have preparations made well beforehand so that the instant a recognized risk occurs, you simply implement the correct plan which you had already developed to handle it right there and then.

For example, having the right material to protect your construction site from the beginning will allow you to avoid losses from the thunderstorm since you will be ready to deal with it.

Also, in case of an IT project, if there is a risk that one of your programming specialists might leave the job, it is wise to have backup specialists ready to take up the job instantly.

Perform Qualitative Risk Analysis Process

Performing Qualitive Risk Analysis involves prioritizing risks by evaluating their probability and impact. It shows you which risks can have the most impact or influence on your project. Here, you will shortlist the most important risks that can affect your project.

There are two key things that you will analyse the risks for.

- The Probability or likelihood that a particular risk will occur
- The Impact that risk can have on the cost, schedule, quality or performance of the project.

Let's discuss probability and impact one by one:

For example, let's say that you're working on a construction project and you're making over 100 different apartment buildings. Think about what are the risks that can occur on that specific project. For example, an environmental disturbance like an earthquake or a thunderstorm could be one of them. So it is useful to consider what is the probability of that thunderstorm occurring while you're actually constructing the buildings.

The second thing you want to consider is if that thunderstorm does occur, then what can be its impact on the project. It may either end up damaging your equipment or it might even delay your schedule.

Similarly, if you're working on developing a software, what are the risks you could encounter? E.g. there could be the risk of data loss. What could be the probability of losing your software product due to faulty memory storage, and how big of an impact/setback would that be for the project.

Organizations use a Probability and Impact Matrix to develop a standardized rating system to evaluate risks.

Risk Probability			
Probability Rating	1	2	3
Probability Rating Interpretation	Low	Medium	High

As you can see, any risks with a rating of 3 is high priority and needs to be taken care of asap, while those with a rating of 1 can be put on the watch list. The watch list contains low priority risks which may possibly become more significant in the future, so they need to be monitored.

Risk Impact (Cost) +/-			
Impact Rating	1	2	3
Impact Rating Interpretation	$1000	$5000	$10000

Similarly, we can evaluate the risk for its impact. In this example, we are observing the impact on Costs. An impact level of 3 will incur a loss of $10,000, if it is a negative risk. If it is a positive risk, this means there is an opportunity for the project e.g. if there is a possibility the price of raw materials goes down and you are able to buy them at a cheaper price, saving you $10,000 compared to what was originally estimated in the project budget.

Therefore, it is important to consider all the different ways in which your project can be impacted by the different risks.

Once you've conducted this Qualitative analysis you will have identified which of the risks are the most important ones that you need to respond to. Then, as a result of the analysis, you're going to shortlist the most important risks which can affect our project.

Perform Quantitative Risk Analysis Process

Quantitative Risk Analysis is performed for risks that need to be understood on a deeper level. It is usually performed for the top risks that you shortlisted earlier during Qualitative Risk Analysis.

Putting it simply, this process quantifies the effect of risks on your project. This is done by giving a numerical value to the risks that you've identified and analysed.

For example, a risk with a rating of 4 according to qualitative analysis, will incur a loss of $20,000.

To evaluate a risk for its effect on the project, you may use the Expected Monetary Value (EMV) method.

EMV = P x I (Probability x Impact)

Let's continue example of having a thunderstorm occur on your bridge construction site.

Let's assume there is a 60% probability of the thunderstorm occurring while the project is being carried out, and you foresee it might cause damage to your equipment. You estimate the impact of the risk to be worth $40,000.

To calculate the EMV of the risk, you will apply the formula:

EMV = P x I

EMV = 60% x $40,000 = 24,000

Hence, a 60 % probability of the thunderstorm occurring would incur damages worth $24000 on the project.

Also, remember that risks can also be positive.

Let's consider that we have to buy construction machinery regularly during the project due to the large demand of work being done. If during the project, there is a possibility that the the prices of the machinery and equipment for building construction will decrease during the second month of the project.

This event will end up saving you money since a price decrease benefits your project by decreasing project costs. If a crane costed $100,000, but if there is a possibility of a price decrease to $80,000, then you will end up saving $20,000.

Hence, in the quantitative analysis process, you will assign more concrete numerical values to the risks you're facing, whether positive, or negative.

Plan Risk Responses Process

Now let's move forward to the plan risk response process. Once you've identified all the top risks you need to develop the risk response plans. The purpose of this plan is to take care of the risks on the project whether they're negative or positive.

A risk response plan contains the specific responses for the risks that can occur on the project.

If it's a negative risk, the risk response plans are meant to get rid of or lessen the impact of the threats which are negative risks.

If it's a positive risk, you want to make sure that you get a hold of it and ensure that you capitalize on it.

For example, in case of a negative risk, if you shortlist a thunderstorm as a high priority risk, what would be a good risk response plan for it?

Possible Risk Response Plans

1. Keep a lookout for risk triggers (early signs of the risk) so that in case you can accurately forecast a specific day for the storm, you can move your equipment inside the warehouse.

A **Risk Trigger** is any sign that a risk is about to occur on the project

2. You may purchase protective waterproof coverings for any sensitive equipment or material you're using for the project and ensure its availability on hand if there is a possibility of an environmental hazard.

On the other hand, if you're dealing with a positive risk or an opportunity e.g. if you know that prices of the raw materials will be cheaper in the third month of the project, then you want to make sure that you purchase the raw material in that specific month so that you can end up decreasing the overall cost of the product.

Implement Risk Response Process

Next is the implement risk response's process. Now that you have the risk responses planned for tackling the specific risks you expect to face, you want to make sure that they're implemented on the project as well.

(Note: **Risk Owners** are people who take up the responsibility to implement a particular risk response plan to take care of a specific risk if it occurs. This can be anyone from the project team or stakeholders.)

Implementing risk responses emphasizes that it is important for the risk owners to uphold their responsibility and to be proactive in implementing the risk responses in order to address the negative risk meaning threats or the opportunities which are the positive risks.

This is how the events will flow:

Once you have identified the risks,

You will then develop the responses for them,

Designate specific people or risk owners who will take on their responsibility to tackle the risks in case they occur on the project.

So what happens when the alarm goes off and a risk becomes likely to occur on the project?

Once the risk trigger has occurred, then the risk owner will implement the risk response plan in order to tackle the risk. It is important to make sure that you tackle it well in time before 1. You lose out on the opportunity if it is a positive risk, or 2. The risk causes damage to the project if it is a negative risk.

Monitor Risks Process

By this point of the project, you have already assigned risk owners and you've put the risk response plans in place. When it comes to monitoring risks, you are mainly responsible for implementing the risk response plans when risks occur, identifying any new risks that can occur on the project, lastly, you are tracking identified risks to see what the likelihood of them is occurring on the project. So, you're taking a proactive approach in protecting and enhancing your project.

To sum it all up, proper risk management not only protect your project from harm (negative risks), moreover, it can also help you in capitalizing on the opportunities (positive risks) that can occur in the environment.

Procurement Management

What is Procurement Management

What are Procurements

Procurement refers to obtaining goods and services through a formal procedure. So, the types of things that are procured includes both goods and services, it's important to make that distinction between the two.

Now let's take an example of each type of different procurement. An example of goods would include procuring a certain type of machinery for your factory. On the other hand, when it comes to procuring services, this would include getting work done through an outsourced supplier. For instance, you could get the design of your website done by outsourcing it to a graphic design company and you could code and program the website by yourself.

Procurement Management

Procurement Management refers to the process of how to acquire products and services from outside the product organization. It helps you in identifying a suitable supplier for getting products and services which are the right fit for your project. It also includes determining whether to acquire them from an external organization or if it is more feasible to get them developed in the house by the project team. Furthermore, it also involves controlling the contract in order to ensure that contractual obligations are performed by the involved parties.

Procurements are mostly managed by a procurement department and it is important to note that the project manager is not expected to manage the procurement process. However, they should be familiar with the procurement process because they are responsible for supporting it. So basically, the project manager does not directly conduct the procurements but in fact as a supporter for procurements while the actual procurements are handled by the procurement department.

Procurement Management involves the following processes:

1. Plan Procurement Management

2. Conduct Procurements

3. Control Procurements

Overview of Procurements on a Project

Before we delve into the processes for procurement management, I'd like to give you a quick overview of what it is all about. So, let's see step by step what happens during procurement management on a project:

When a project is being planned, the scope of work, i.e. the work required to complete the project is analyzed.

Then, it is determined whether the work required on the project will be completed internally by the project team and internal resources OR whether all or any part of it needs to be outsourced to an external organization.

This process we just discussed is known as a Make or Buy Analysis, where we decide whether to do the project by ourselves (within the organization) and whether we need to outsource some part of the work (to an external partner or contactor)

Once the Make or Buy decision is complete, the project manager helps create a procurement management plan and procurement statement of work

- The Project Management Plan details how procurement will take place on the project
- The Procurement statement of work describes the work to be done by the seller

The Procurement Manager then determines

- The type of contract to be used
- and the type of Procurement Document to be used

Procurement Documents include:

- an RFQ, which is a Request for quotation
- an IFB, which is an Invitation for Bid
- and an RFP, which is a Request for proposal

The procurement manager creates the procurement documents. These documents are meant to help facilitate contain information on what kind of work is required to be done on the project. The documents also contain information on the Terms of the contract. The procurement statement of work along with the contract terms are combined to form the finalized procurement documents which are sent to the seller.

Procurement Documents = Statement of Work + Contract Terms

The documents are sent to the prospective sellers from whom you want to acquire services or goods.

The Sellers then review the documents to understand the requirements of the buyer. This review helps them understand clearly what sort of work the buyer requires from them.

The review process also helps the seller assess the risks of the project before sending the proposal to the buyer.

The Seller then prepares a proposal and sends it to the buyer.

Also, do note that you must take into account the time it will take the Sellers to prepare the proposal to maintain a realistic timeline. The time taken to prepare the proposal should be included the project schedule.

Next, let's learn what happens now that the seller has sent their proposal document to the buyer:

The Buyer then reviews the proposals and uses different methods to shortlist and select a seller. The criteria for selecting a seller can involve different variables such as cost, experience, skill level etc., so you choose the one whoever fits your criteria based on your requirements and what you are able to offer for their services.

Once the seller is selected, the contract is signed.

The signing of the contract does not mark the end of the procurement, in fact, now that the contract is signed, it needs to be managed and controlled.

Managing and Controlling the Contract refers to ensuring that all the requirements stated in the contract are fulfilled. It also involves implementing changes on the contract. In case changes are required on the procurement work, The Project Manager can refer to the Contract Change Control System. This is the system that manages changes on the contract, so you can keep track of previous and updated work done by the seller.

Finally, once the work has been completed and the seller has delivered their service, the procurement will be closed.

How to Perform Procurement Management

Plan Procurement Management Process

Now we're going to learn about the different processes in procurement management. Please do keep in mind that we're talking about this process from the perspective of the buyer. Meaning that you are purchasing products or services for your project.

The first process is called Plan procurement management. Think of this process as if you are going for shopping for your product. It is in this process that you will decide as to what products or services you require to get the project done. You also need to decide whether you should make those products or services by yourself or whether you should acquire them from the outside.

In this process you will create a very important document by the name of the procurement statement of work. This document includes all the work and activities the seller is required to complete for the buyer. For example, if you're buying some sort of a product or services for your project, then this is the document which will detail all of the work that needs to be done by the person that you're purchasing it from.

Therefore, it includes all the actual work done and performed by the seller regarding the procurement.

Furthermore, this document also includes fulfilling other requirements apart from the core work required. For example, if you require the seller to make any sort of progress/status reports or you have a criterion for how to conduct communications/meetings, then that information should also be included in the procurement statement of work. Hence, the procurement statement of work includes all the work that needs to be done by the seller for the buyer.

You will also need to create the procurement documents. This includes the guidelines, background information on the project and the selection criteria for the vendors.

During this process you will also conduct the make or buy analysis. During this analysis you will decide whether to do the project work all by yourself, meaning do you want to make the product or service which needs to be used on the project, or are you going to outsource all of the work or maybe part of the work.

In what scenario would you want to outsource the work or buy a product/service from external sellers?

This is usually done when you want to decrease your own risk, because every company is not good at everything. For example, you may be good at product development but maybe you're not that great at supply chain management. So in that case, you would outsource the supply chain and work to an outsourced supplier. An interesting case to notice would be that Apple plans its Product Design/Development and Branding in the US while it outsources the actual manufacturing and assembly of its products to China.

In what situation would you want to do the work yourself?

You would choose to do this in a situation where you want to retain more copyright control over your product or service in case you don't want your private information going out into the market.

Conduct Procurements Process

Next let's look at the conduct procurement process.

Now this is the actual process where you will be conducting the procurements, it includes sending the procurement statement of work and the procurement documents to the sellers.

It also involves answering any questions which the sellers may ask. Then, once the sellers have submitted their responses, you will review them.

After that, based on your selection criteria, you would end up finalizing and selecting a seller who fulfils your criteria the best.

Control Procurements Process

Next, we're going to look at how are you going to control the procurements.

Controlling procurements is all about how you are going to manage the contractual relationship between the buyer and the seller.

The major objective here is that you need to make sure that all the terms which are contained in the contract are fulfilled by both parties.

During this process, as a project manager, you may be involved in several different tasks. You may be involved in authorizing payments to the seller and reviewing the invoices received from the seller. You would be monitoring the cost, schedule and the scope of the procurement. You will also be performing audits and inspections of the seller's processes and the deliverables which they give you.

You will be analysing what is and what is not contained within the contract. Furthermore, you will hold performance review meetings with the seller. You will be managing the changes for procurements. And finally, you will be reporting on the performance for both parties i.e. the buyer, as well as the seller.

Hence, control procurement process is all about making sure that the work that is supposed to be done on the procurements by the seller is going according to plan.

Stakeholder Management

What is Stakeholder Management

Stakeholder Management involves identifying people who can be impacted by the project. Secondly, it also involves understanding their expectations, requirements and influence on the product. As a project manager, you will develop stakeholder management strategies to keep the stakeholders engaged and interested in the project. This includes continuously communicating with them, meeting their needs and addressing their issues.

Stakeholder management needs to be maintained throughout a project's life. The needs of different stakeholders need to be taken into account in order to make the project a success. We should remember that it is very necessary to determine the expectations, requirements and influence of the stakeholders in order to properly manage their involvement on the project. If not handled properly, unsatisfied stakeholders may possibly create hurdles for the project.

Who are internal and external stakeholders

Now let's learn about who exactly are stakeholders. These are people who can be positively or negatively impacted by the project, meaning the project can either benefit them, or possibly harm/interfere with their work.

Internal stakeholders include people who are directly working on the project, such as your project team. Technical experts are one of the more important stakeholders since they possess expertise on getting the project work done. This may include e.g. engineers, IT specialists etc. Internal stakeholders also include the people working in different departments of the organization, e.g. marketing, finance, supply chain etc. It may also include the different functional managers and the employees of the organization from whom you would need to make requests for resources regarding your project (For instance, you might need to request Functional managers to share their team members for a certain amount of time if they have a special skillset you could use on your project, e.g. a multilingual engineer who speaks Chinese and English fluently)

On the other hand, the project may also include people who are outside your organization, this includes the external stakeholders such as the raw material suppliers, external contractors and agencies that your organization is working with.

Stakeholder Management Processes

Stakeholder Management involves the following processes:

- Identify Stakeholders
- Plan Stakeholder Management
- Manage Stakeholder Engagement
- Monitor Stakeholder Engagement

How to Perform Stakeholder Management

Identify Stakeholders Process

This is the process in which you will identify all the different people and organizations who are involved and impacted by the project. Furthermore, it is also important to collect all the information regarding the stakeholder's involvement, interest and the positive/negative impact that they can have on the project.

Hence, after identifying stakeholders, you will prepare a detailed list of stakeholders. Also, it is important to conduct a stakeholder analysis whereby you will evaluate the influence of different people involve on the project. You will then compile all the information regarding stakeholders in a document known as a stakeholder register. The stakeholder register is a document which contains all the information regarding stakeholders involved on the project including requirements, role, level of influence etc.

Another important thing to remember is that stakeholders are identified in the initiating process. So this means that you will identify as many stakeholders as possible during the beginning of the project.

Plan Stakeholder Engagement Process

Next, you have to plan stakeholder engagement. At this point, you will have an exhaustive list of all the stakeholders involved on the project.

In this process, you will develop the strategies to engage stakeholders across the entire duration of the project. Relationships with stakeholders are important for any project. Whether you are dealing with an external stakeholder like a supplier or whether you're dealing with an internal stakeholder like the engineering team, you need to make sure that you have strong relationships with them. Having positive relationships with stakeholders can help you avoid problems and get your work done faster with relative ease.

Therefore, figure out who exactly are the stakeholders, how will the project affect them, how can you fulfil their expectations, and what can you do to engage and communicate with them. The goal is to develop a healthy relationship across the entire duration of the project, whereby the involved parties can reap good benefits by working together. A good starting point for building relationships is simply to get to know them, talk to them, learn about their priorities from the project, and then see if you can cater to them.

Manage Stakeholder Engagement Process

Managing stakeholder engagement is the process of communicating with the stakeholders to gain their commitment and support. One of the main priorities of any project manager involves gaining the support of all of the different types of stakeholders and decreasing their resistance to the project.

There might be some stakeholders who might not be too happy with the project. For example, If you are borrowing resources from the engineering team for your project, then the functional manager of engineering might not be too happy that you are borrowing his resources. So you need to make sure that you develop a good relationship with that functional manager to alleviate any negative outcomes, or else he/she could possibly refrain from sharing his resources at critical points of your project.

How can we address this situation and prepare for it? It is important to develop a positive relationship and understand their worries and concerns. If the manager is worried his team would be distracted from their main responsibilities and core work, then you could develop a specific schedule of where and when exactly you would require resources from his/her team. You could also be proactive by ensuring there is little overlap between the engineering teams own high priority commitments and the time when you would require them to work on your own project. This would help alleviate his/her concerns since you addressed the uncertainty about the availability of his/her team members.

Hence, such positive actions towards relationship building will help you in easily acquiring the resources that you require and getting your project work done in an efficient way. By having a strong relationship with different stakeholders, you can ensure that your project will be successful.

Monitor Stakeholder Engagement Process

In Monitor Stakeholder Engagement, you will observe and track your relationships with the stakeholders. Across the duration of your project, you need to evaluate what exactly is the status of your relationship, are they satisfied or are they dissatisfied with the project?

If they are not happy with the project, then what exactly do we need to do to bring them on board. The key is that you need to make sure you identify any issues at the earliest, so you can solve the problems as early as possible. The earlier you spot the problems, the better it is. Once you've identified any problems you need to make sure that you make the right changes to improve communications understanding and the engagement of the stakeholders on the project.

Thank You

Congratulations!!

By now, you've absorbed the core fundamentals of project management and have a top-level view of the most important aspects to take care of while managing projects.

Anytime you set out to manage a project, go over the knowledge areas and start thinking about what are steps you need to take for your project when it comes to Integration, Scope, Risks, Costs etc.

My sincerest hope is for you to make your professional and personal life more efficient and productive, so that you make the most out of whatever you choose to do.

I wish you the best in everything you do and everywhere you go.

Umer W.

Made in United States
Orlando, FL
13 February 2023

29957523R00085